The SHAKARIAN Legacy

How A Humble Dairyman Inspired The World!

DEMOS SHAKARIAN

CYNTHIA SHAKARIAN

Foreword by **KENNETH COPELAND**

Published By
SHAKARIAN COLLECTIVE

This book is dedicated to my grandfather,
Demos Shakarian.
He was an amazing man with a vision from God,
who followed his heart and changed nations.
This Stetson-hat wearing man
touched my heart forever.
He always had endless time for me
no matter how busy he was.

I was his "Cynthia-jan," which in Armenian
is a term of endearment meaning "Cynthia darling."
I felt incredible love and affirmation
from him in everything I did,
well, most things anyway!
He was my true example of pure unconditional love.

This man, my grandfather . . . "My Bobby!"

Introduction

*T*he *Shakarian Legacy* pays tribute to and is inspired by my grandfather, Demos Shakarian. It paves the way so future generations can learn about his inspirational life story. This book was written from my heart and reflects my viewpoint as his granddaughter. Remembering the times I spent with my grandparents, and the stories they shared with me.

He called himself an ordinary dairyman, a helper, and an encourager, but I and many others saw him as extraordinary. Fulfilling his purpose and his destiny; he touched the world with God's love by following the leading of the Holy Spirit.

My grandfather profoundly impacted his generation. Still, many people have not had the opportunity to know him. My desire is for today's and future generations to also have the opportunity to be impacted by his life. So I am continuing his legacy by sharing my memories of him. These stories demonstrate the examples he set and the values he represented.

Grandfather was a humble man. A successful California dairy farmer by vocation, his love for the Lord called him to reach beyond the fences of his expanding dairy farm, to change and impact the lives of people across the globe. He influenced me by virtue of his example. I was able to experience the way he lived his life and touched the lives of people worldwide.

My desire in writing this book is to inspire many to listen more intently and have the same kind of steadfast faith to —
Find Your Purpose, Enlarge Your Vision & Pursue Your Destiny!

With Much Love,

Cynthia Rene'e Shakarian

Foreword
by Kenneth Copeland

"Cynthia dear girl, you're anointed to do this! Your Granddad was a GREAT BLESSING to Gloria and me, and opened his heart to us in the early years of our ministry. Such a man of integrity and devotion to the Lord Jesus, he set the standards high for the rest of us to follow. He and my spiritual father, Oral Roberts, being such close friends together blazed the trails which have become today's highways we're traveling on in this great outpouring. My, how I do miss them!

The Shakarian Legacy is absolutely wonderful! Remembering the exciting times we all had in the meetings and conventions. For those of you who missed it all, read the book and enjoy the times! Thank you Cynthia, for doing this very special work!

JESUS IS LORD!"

— **Kenneth Copeland** • Founder / Kenneth Copeland Ministries

Contents

Acknowledgments

"Wow, isn't this wonderful! Jesus is Here!
I think God wants to show Southern California, and from here to
the world, that He is ALIVE! Jesus is ALIVE!"
— **Demos Shakarian** • October 4, 1981

LISTED IN ORDER OF APPEARANCE

In gratitude, I thank those who so eloquently contributed their memories of my grandfather, Demos Shakarian. What a joy for me to read your words and see how far my grandfather's legacy reached and the momentum has not stopped!

"The Shakarian Legacy is absolutely wonderful! Your Granddad was a GREAT BLESSING to Gloria and me. Such a man of integrity and devotion to the Lord Jesus, he set the standards high for the rest of us to follow. Cynthia dear girl, you're anointed to do this! JESUS IS LORD!"
— **Kenneth Copeland** • Founder / Kenneth Copeland Ministries

"May your book inspire its readers through the powerful legacy your grandfather left. Cynthia, thank you for embarking on this important project!"
— **Joseph Prince** • Pastor / New Creation Church, Singapore

"Demos was a man filled with the Holy Spirit and a giant of faith. His life and work has inspired me to carry the Gospel across the whole earth."
— **Reinhard Bonnke** • Evangelist / Christ For All Nations

"Demos had a great impact in our lives. He was a good friend to my husband, John Osteen. Because of him, we went all over the nation preaching."
— **Dodie Osteen** • Co-Founder / Lakewood Church

"Demos Shakarian massively and positively impacted the lives of many Nigerian businessmen and women across our great nation of Nigeria."
— **David Oyedepo** • Bishop / Living Faith Church Worldwide

"Demos created such a warm group of businessmen who walked in the love of God."
— **Mary Hudson** • President / Arise International

"Attending my grandparents' church (Hamas Shakarian Kardashian and Tom Kardashian) I recall Rose playing the piano. Demos was my Dad's first cousin. His kindness overflowed but so did his Dad's, my great-uncle Isaac."
— **Barbara Kardashian Carr** • Demos' second cousin

"Demos ignited businessmen around the world and brought the Holy Spirit to them."
— **Paul Dhinakaran, Ph.D.** • President / Jesus Calls International, India

"Demos' life showed me that God exists and His miracles are real today."
— **Tony Jansezian** • Fellow Armenian from Jerusalem, Israel

"Demos believed God's power could impact every person in society as it is not limited to an expression within the four walls of the church."
— **Guillermo Maldonado** • Apostle / King Jesus International Ministry

"The story of Demos Shakarian will encourage you, challenge you and inspire you."
— **Rod Parsley** • Pastor / World Harvest Church, Host of *Breakthrough*

"When I came to faith, the spiritual giants of that era included Demos Shakarian. His infectious and vibrant faith inspired my own."
— **Chris Mitchell** • Middle East Bureau Chief / *CBN News*

"Demos took the vision God gave him and impacted men, cities, and nations."
— **Carman Licciardello** • Recording Artist, Multiple GMA Dove Award Winner

"God took a dairy farmer and energized a man's vision to penetrate the scope of the business world."
— **Jack Hayford** • Chancellor / *The King's University*

"May the story of this precious man stir you to reach for more!"
— **Nancy Dufresne** • Dufresne Ministries

"Demos' organization was one of the most powerful moves of God on the planet and gathered Christians from every nation and denomination!"
— **Rick Joyner** • Author / "The Final Quest" series

"Demos Shakarian is a name which will be honored throughout history because he greatly exalted the name above all names, Jesus Christ!"
— **Patricia King** • Co-Founder / XPmedia

"Demos gave me my first opportunity to speak. God really used Demos Shakarian to impact the world for Jesus!"
—**Sid Roth** • Host / *It's Supernatural!*

"I loved Demos Shakarian. I'm excited something new is happening with Demos' vision. I'm glad Cynthia Shakarian is listening to the Holy Spirit."
— **Jerry Savelle** • Founder / Jerry Savelle Ministries International

"Demos touched my life in a profound way! His legacy continues today. Only eternity will reveal the countless lives he touched for God's glory."
— **Benny Hinn** • Pastor / Benny Hinn Ministries

"Demos and Rose had the ability to see potential in a person's call."
— **Robin Harfouche** • Global Revival

"Demos Shakarian represented the scriptural truth which wealth is gained by following the principles of economics. This is of God."
— **Noel Jones** • Bishop / City of Refuge, Featured on *Preachers of L.A.*

"Honoring our past opens up our future. Without Demos, I'm not sure I would have recognized and nurtured the gift within me."
— **Chuck D. Pierce** • President / Glory of Zion International

"There would be little emphasis on 'market-place ministry' without Demos' organization building a coalition of business owners and entrepreneurs."
— **Mark Chironna** • Pastor / Church on the Living Edge

"Demos lived by principles of character and integrity."
— **Nancy Alcorn** • President / Mercy Ministries

"I thank God for your grandparents. Their vision literally shook the world. How blessed you are Cynthia to be walking in a generational blessing."
— **Marilyn Hickey** • President / Marilyn Hickey Ministries

"Sometimes you can get so busy with what you're expected to do, you can easily miss what you were born to do!"
— **Cynthia Shakarian** • Inspirational Author / International Speaker

"Taking God's truth to businesses was effective and appealing. Sharing how God's kingdom impacts life where people live, in the marketplace."
— **Gary Keesee** • Pastor, Host / *Fixing the Money Thing*

"Demos Shakarian was nothing less than a walking legend. In the world of Christianity, he is one of the greatest leaders in the last 100 years."
— **Tim Storey** • Interviewed by Oprah Winfrey / OWN's *Super Soul Sunday,* Speaker

"Through most of this remarkable-though-humble man's life, everyone he touched was impacted with a love which defies description."
— **Pat Boone** • Singer, Actor, Entertainer

"Demos showed you can be unique and yet powerful in your own arena of life. I'm thankful for the vision to take the gospel to Hollywood!"
— **Ruckins McKinley, D.D.** • Author / *The Sound*

"My dad, Kenneth E. Hagin was involved with Demos and esteemed him highly. I know my dad was glad to call Demos his friend."
— **Kenneth E. Hagin, Jr** • Rhema Ministries / Kenneth Hagin Ministries

"Everyone has a dream, but there are those who believe their dreams are really God's ideas. Demos was such a man. Cynthia now carries a prophetic passion for the continuation of her grandfather's vision."
— **Gary Zamora** • Pastor / Gary Zamora Ministries

"Demos was a great help to my dad from the beginning of Oral Roberts University!"
— **Richard Roberts** • Oral Roberts Ministries

"Demos' platform of marketplace leaders and entrepreneurs experienced the message of Jesus. Without him, the world would not be the same!"
— **Samuel Rodriguez** • Pres. / National Hispanic Christian Leadership Conference

"The Lord used Demos to launch me into the purpose and plan of God for my life."
— **Norvel Hayes** • Norvel Hayes Ministries

"I can't thank God enough for this wonderful man. I'm excited his granddaughter Cynthia has written this book. I believe you will be blessed by it!"
— **Jesse Duplantis** • Founder / Jesse Duplantis Ministries

"His whole life was working on the dairy farm and building *Reliance Dairy*. It was Demos Shakarian's passion. But spreading God's love, that was his heart! His greatest desire was to follow his dream and fulfill his purpose!"
— **Cynthia Shakarian** • Inspirational Author / International Speaker

"Demos blazed a trail! Living in a very racially divided society, I saw people from all backgrounds, colors, and denominations worshipping in the same room!"
— **Judy Jacobs** • Co-Pastor / Dwelling Place Church International

"Demos urged businessmen to allow the Holy Spirit to become their permanent partner in business. God was blessing businesses!"
— **Ralph Wilkerson** • Founder / Melodyland Christian Center

"Thank you Demos, for the powerful ministry which was our lifeline to the Spirit-filled ministry in the 1960's!"
— **Larry Stockstill** • Pastor / Bethany World Prayer Center

"We sang 'Riding the Range for Jesus' for this true cowboy. When singing, 'His Banner Over Me is Love,' it was Demos who showed it without restraint."
— **Jerry and Sandi Barnard** • Pastors / The Horizon Church

"Demos was led of the Holy Spirit and didn't have any other agenda. He was a marvelous example. We need more like him!"
— **Paul and Joyce Toberty** • Authors / *A Nation Born in a Day*

"There may be no greater testament to a person's life than to see their vision continue. Cynthia has taken the baton which Demos passionately carried bringing the message to a new generation with relevance and a compelling new voice."
— **Joe Ninowski, Jr** • Producer / *Daystar* Television Network

"Demos had the wisdom to not only take the gospel outside the four walls of the church but to also break down denominational boundaries."
— **Scott Wead** • Pastor / Life House Worship Center

"Demos impacted greatly the lives of my husband and myself. We ventured outside our denominational walls largely due to Demos."
— **Billye Brim** • Billye Brim Ministries / Prayer Mountain in the Ozarks

"I had the amazing privilege of attending Demos' Convention with Oral Roberts, Kathryn Kuhlman, Kenneth E. Hagin, Kenneth Copeland (my dad) and Andre Crouch. I do not exaggerate when I say the power could be felt in the parking lot!"
— **Terri Copeland Pearsons** • Senior Pastor / Eagle Mountain Church

"I observed Demos separate himself from things not in line with God's Word!"
— **Nicky Cruz** • Subject of the movie *The Cross and the Switchblade*

"I attribute my initial separation into ministry to Demos! He touched his generation in a massive way!"
— **Kim Clement** • Founder, Prophet / Kim Clement Center

"At Demos Shakarian's conventions, I met successful businessmen who found a greater purpose to their lives than just making money."
— **Bob Harrison** • Founder / Increase

"His example of listening to the voice of the Holy Spirit was inspiring."
— **Bayless Conley** • Pastor / Cottonwood Church

"Demos was undoubtedly 'one-of-a-kind.' One of God's choice generals."
— **Ken and Annie Schisler** • Face To Face Ministry

"Demos Shakarian made a huge impact in New York City. He was authentic in his pursuit of God and in his relationships with friends!"
— **Arlene Vikse Del Rio** • Pastor / Abounding Grace Ministries

"It's one thing to have a great vision and another to obey the vision!!"
— **Glenda Jackson** • Niece of Maria Woodworth-Etter, Glenda Jackson Ministries

"I shared with Demos that we were interested in his building. He said he had dedicated it to God. On Easter, our first service was held."
— **Jeff Johnson** • Senior Pastor / Calvary Chapel Downey

"Cynthia, your granddad Demos was a great leader. Millions of people were blessed because of him. I am proud to say I am one of them!"
— **Roosevelt (Rosey) Grier** • All-Pro New York Giants

"I was honored to speak at Demos' Convention. The Holy Spirit was moving to love God and one another; a message that Demos lived."
— **James Robison** • Founder / LIFE Outreach International

"It's your commitment and confidence; your values of faith, family, and freedom which make us know Americans are a good and decent people, who inspire us to believe America can be a great nation."
— **President Ronald Reagan** • 40th President of the United States: July 5, 1984

"Demos' vision of reaching men and women was unstoppable."
— **Ronn Haus** • Pastor / President, TV 42

"Mr. Demos Shakarian, You have reached an important milestone in your life, and I join with you in that celebration."
— **President Bill Clinton** • 42nd President of the United States: July 3, 1993

"Cynthia, it is important that people do not forget your grandfather. He brought pastors together and united businessmen, and the Lord is using you to keep the vision Alive!"
— **Howard Richardson** • Pastor, Prophet / Gates of Glory

"Cynthia, by meeting many Diplomats, Presidents and Heads of State you will reach nations and countries. You are a visionary, a humanitarian and philanthropist. What you are Cynthia Shakarian, is one of God's own Ambassadors for humanity."
— **Al G. Forniss** • Apostle / Al Forniss Ministries

The SHAKARIAN Legacy

How A Humble Dairyman Inspired The World!

DEMOS SHAKARIAN

CHAPTER ONE

A Special Night
with My Grandparents

❦

I was eight years old, curled up in a huge overstuffed wingback chair made with soft, elegant fabric. Feeling warm and cozy, wearing pink flannel pajamas and soft fuzzy slippers, I watched my grandfather's every move. From across the room, I could see everything that was happening. The chair was situated with an around-the-room view in the massive living room of my grandparent's beautiful hotel suite.

This particular night my grandmother Rose, whom I called "Momie" (an affectionate term for grandmother), had already gone to bed for the night exhausted from a busy day. Grandfather, on the other hand, was more of a late-night person. I was still wide awake and too excited to think about sleep. This was a special night because I was spending it with my grandparents!

The hotel suite was buzzing with activity, and I was fascinated. The evening meeting of my grandfather's convention had ended, and guests had come from near and far. My eyes jumped from one person to the next as the room held so many interesting people. There was a woman wearing a black tailored dress with long white satin gloves and a hat which appeared to be made entirely of feathers. To me, it looked like she had a big bird sitting on her head! Another man was smiling and talking, wearing the shiniest shoes I had ever seen. It felt like I was watching a movie with all the characters playing their parts.

I knew him as "Bobby," a term of endearment used for "grandfather."

The world knew Grandfather as Demos Shakarian, Founder, and President of Full Gospel Business Men's Fellowship International (FGBMFI). I knew him as "Bobby," a term of endearment many Armenians used for grandfather. Through all the exhilaration and energy of the evening, I was most excited just to be there with my Bobby.

I didn't know what my grandfather was to the world, but as I grew up, I began to see lives were changed by the love of God in him. How great was he to always make me feel special, no matter how important the person was beside him. He allowed me to be his granddaughter, and he my grandfather.

The telephone seemed to continually ring at their home with calls from around the world. It appeared to me, a great variety of people from all walks of life hungered for his attention: politicians, dignitaries, businessmen, and celebrities.

OBSERVING GRANDFATHER'S KINDNESS

That evening in the hotel suite was no different. Sitting with my legs tucked underneath me, I gazed across the huge living room filled with beautiful furniture and windows draped in velvet. Though even being in these elegant surroundings didn't distract me from my grandfather. Some guests were standing together in small groups talking, while others were eating the sandwiches, salads, and array of desserts set up on tables for everyone to enjoy. Grandfather took time for each person, showing such kindness in his own gentle way. Though the hotel suite was packed with people, he did not seem hurried as he cordially welcomed additional guests.

Every so often he would look over at me and give me a smile as if to make sure all was well. When he walked by where I was sitting, he made a point to introduce me to whomever he was talking. To my delight, he always included something very complimentary about me along with his introduction. He had a way of making me feel special, and years later I discovered he made others feel special as well. While my grandfather seemed *My grandmother Rose, whom I called "Momie."* gracious and unencumbered by the clock, I was looking forward to some alone time with my Bobby. Glancing around the room, I forced my eyes to stay open. Could it be? It looked like the very last man was leaving.

Reflecting on these memories now, I can see my innocence prevented me from comprehending the full magnitude of what was happening around me. I realize now these precious men and women had traveled from around the world to attend my grandfather's convention, held in the hotel's Grand Ballroom many floors below. It was not until much later in my life that I became aware of just how he and his organization would one day impact the world!

> "God used your grandfather mightily to impact countless lives. Thank you for embarking on this important project. May your book bless and inspire its readers in their faith through the powerful legacy your grandfather left behind."
> — **Joseph Prince** • Pastor / New Creation Church, Singapore

NEVER TOO BUSY FOR ONE MORE

"Thank you for coming, it means so much to Rose and me," I heard my grandfather saying to the last guest. "Will I see you in the morning at the men's breakfast meeting?" It was always a regular part of every convention. I could feel my eyes getting heavier as I heard the last guest exclaim, "I wouldn't miss it!"

Then as my eyes began to close in defeat, I heard the door shut. My eyes popped wide open, just in time to see Grandfather turn around. Our eyes connected, I could see the surprise on his face as he assumed I had been sleeping. His shock at seeing me awake was followed by that unforgettable grin as he walked across the room to sit by me. Then, the unthinkable happened: a knock at the door.

My grandfather turned around, walked toward the door and opened it. There in front of him stood a man who appeared to be very excited. He was short, dressed in black pants, a black vest, and a white shirt. I heard him introduce himself.

Grandfather had a way of making everyone feel special.

"Pardon me, sir," said the man. "I'm a bellman here at the hotel and I heard you were staying with us. I've been waiting for your guests to leave because I had to tell you something. Your organization has meant so much to me since I accepted Jesus into my life at one of your meetings."

LASTING IMPRESSIONS

What happened next is one of my favorite memories of my Bobby and was the inspiration which inspired me to write this book!

My grandfather swung open his hotel door and invited the bellman inside as if he were greeting one of the invited dignitaries. It was quite late, and I was sure Grandfather was beginning to tire. I know I was. Yet, there he stood, asking the bellman to come in and have a seat.

As I listened to the bellman share his story, I became interested too. Seeing my grandfather taking the time to speak with him and hearing how his life had been transformed in one of Grandfather's meetings, I couldn't help but share in the bellman's joy. I understood then just a fraction of my Bobby's heart. The bellman was beaming when he left. "Just wait until I tell my family I talked to Demos Shakarian!" he exclaimed, before thanking Grandfather and enthusiastically walking down the hall.

My Bobby quickly turned and walked towards me, as he sat next to me, his large hand lovingly pinched my cheek. Though I enjoyed conversing with my grandfather, this night I focused on his kindness towards the stranger who knocked on the door. I will never forget his loving response to him.

Wow, that was the moment I began to see how Grandfather was touching and changing lives. I realize now this was the inception of his influence in my life!

"Demos Shakarian was a man filled with the Holy Spirit and a giant of faith. I met him the first time in South Africa, and we became instant friends. His ministry had rapidly spread all over the world, and multitudes of business people found Jesus as their Savior. I saw these branches wherever I went: Europe, Asia, Australia, Africa... Demos invited me to be the keynote speaker in Melbourne, Australia. I spent high-quality time with this great man of God.

His life and work has blessed and inspired me to carry the
burning torch of the Gospel across the whole earth!"
— **Reinhard Bonnke** • Evangelist / Christ for All Nations

REFLECTING ON THE LOVE

While waiting for friends to join me for breakfast at a restaurant in Newport Coast, California, I found myself gazing out over
the Pacific Ocean. The water appeared exceptionally blue, and I
felt incredibly peaceful. Though a chill was in the air, it wasn't
the coffee I was sipping which gave me warmth, but rather all
the wonderful memories running through my mind. The flash-
backs of my grandfather were exceptionally vivid because I was
in the midst of writing my book. As I placed my coffee cup down,
I couldn't help but feel excitement knowing soon others would
also be experiencing my very special time with a very special
man: "my Bobby."

Some people may ask why after all this time I wrote about
my grandfather. It's because I believe his vision which was
instilled in me at an early age, is still so
significant today. He could see more in
What happened next people than they saw in themselves.
inspired me to He recognized their potential and
write this book! purpose and found ways to encourage
their growth. My hope is for us all to realize our dream which
we were born to achieve on this earth. No matter what your
God-given special purpose is, you can have the steadfast faith
to fulfill your vision like Grandfather fulfilled his.

As a businessman, a farmer and a man with a Divine destiny,
Grandfather sowed seeds of love and encouragement in the

lives of businessmen and World Leaders alike. Many of whom went on to do great things and make a difference for eternity. What if he would have given up? Instead, he persisted, thereby affecting countless people across the globe.

What makes his story so amazing is that along with his victories, he had disappointments and struggles too. Though this book is filled

> *I began to see Grandfather was touching and changing lives!*

with words from wonderful people speaking about what he accomplished, my grandfather stood out because he never sought fame or recognition . . . he was a humble dairyman with a big dream!

A FRIEND FROM HOUSTON

I recall one afternoon sitting at my grandmother's kitchen table eating shakar lokum; I can smell those Armenian butter cookies now. They were primarily made of butter and sugar which my grandmother used to cut into diamond-shaped treats.

The phone rang and after Momie hung up, she told me their friend from Houston, Texas had just arrived in town and was on his way to meet with my grandfather. That friend was John Osteen, Joel Osteen's father. In later years he would speak at many of my grandfather's conventions.

At the time I did not recognize the name, but I came to

> *This was the inception of his influence in my life.*

realize what a precious friendship they shared, which made this beautiful note from Dodie Osteen, John's widow, so special to me.

"Demos Shakarian had a great impact on our lives. He was a good friend to my husband, John Osteen. When John first received the Baptism in the Holy Ghost and learned about speaking in tongues and healing, our denomination did not understand, and he resigned.

Demos let us use their huge blow-up Tent, and that's when Lakewood Church began in 1959. John went all over the nation preaching the Good News about Jesus, and it was because of Demos Shakarian. Our children were young but we all have wonderful memories of him.

Thank God for Demos!"

— **Dodie Osteen** • Co-founder / Lakewood Church

IT ALL STARTED IN ARMENIA!

The Bible, which translates to "The Breath of God." Though I cherished listening to my grandparents share all of their stories, I particularly enjoyed hearing about my distant relatives in a far-off land. They lived long ago in a little town called Kara Kala, in a country I could only imagine; Armenia!

Armenia was the first nation in the world to decree Christianity as their state religion in 301 A.D. It was two of the Biblical disciples, Bartholomew and Thaddeus who first brought Christianity to Armenia many years earlier. They shared their faith and baptized the people. In fact, the first book ever written using the Armenian alphabet was the Bible, which translates to "The Breath of God." It's been said that after the Great Flood, Noah's Ark came to rest on a mountain called Mount Ararat. Nestled at the base of this mountain is found a small town called Kara Kala.

Grandfather painted in my mind a picturesque image of our

ancestor's village. It sounded so quaint and nostalgic. I envisioned it as belonging in an old movie.

I had seen advertisements for movies which showed scenery very different from that of my hometown in Southern California. I wondered, *is that what Kara Kala looked like?* I was allowed to watch only *Shirley Temple* and *Disney* films, but I daydreamed of watching other movies as well if only to see more images of this picturesque town. I wanted not just to see the town but also to *feel* what it was like to live there.

As I grew older, my mind began changing the scenery until one day I imagined Kara Kala looked like a town from *Fiddler on the Roof.* I wanted to see all the people at the foot of the mountain including, the ladies hanging their laundry on clotheslines behind their farmhouses and weathered barns. While the men covered with dust and sweat from a long day's work, returned home to unbridle their horses and share the evening meal with their families. I would imagine a sun setting on this little town while hearing a song being sung like, "Tra-di-tion! Tradition!"

THE BOY PROPHET

Kara Kala's best-known resident was named Efim Gerasemovitch Klubniken. I was unable to pronounce his name as a little girl, or even now. Fortunately, he was known as "the Boy Prophet." The first of several prophetic events which would profoundly impact my family's history happened around 1852.

The Boy Prophet and his family were from Russia and settled in Kara Kala. His family was poor, and he was considered illiterate. He had never seen a map, and he did not know anything about geography. All of which, made his abilities even more supernatural! Very early in his life, he recognized the voice of the Lord and spent much time in prayer. It did not take long for news to spread throughout Kara Kala about his extended prayer vigils and his unusual commitment to hearing from the Lord. He was known to go on long fasts as his hours of prayer expanded to several days.

THE VISION AND PROPHECY

At the age of eleven, this Boy Prophet had a vision as he was praying and fasting for many days in his families little house. This vision came in the form of shapes he had never seen before and could not decipher, though he recognized their importance. As he sat at the family dinner table, he began to draw what he had seen in his visions. This painstaking process lasted a full seven days. During this time he neither ate nor slept while he continued to draw, which later would be recognized as charts and maps.

The map depicted a coastline of the Atlantic Ocean.

When the Boy Prophet's vision was complete, his parents took the drawings into the village to find someone who could interpret them. When a few people in Kara Kala saw what he had drawn, they could not believe their eyes. Everything he had written was in Russian! As each word was read, the message became clear. It was a warning from God with instructions for the citizens of Kara Kala about an event which would happen in the future. His vision described a massacre of hundreds of thousands of men, women, and children. It foretold of how the Armenians would be overrun. The vision warned Armenians they must flee to survive. It told of a land across the sea where they would be safe.

The villagers were astonished! He had also sketched a map detailing the land where the Armenians should go. The map depicted a body of water and a coastline of the Atlantic Ocean, which was the east coast of the United States of America. Some villagers disregarded the vision, assuming he was nothing more than an illiterate con-artist pretending to have a supernatural connection to God. Fortunately, most of the villagers in Kara Kala had known Efim, the Boy Prophet, his entire life and they knew they were looking at a prophecy. How else could this illiterate boy have drawn this map and written these words, if it were not a message straight from God? They believed God had chosen this boy as His messenger.

> "Blessed will be the offspring of those who are in obedience. They will be a blessing to the nations!"

The written prophecy did not stop with the instructions to flee across the Atlantic to America at the appointed time. The citizens who left Kara Kala and the surrounding towns were to continue past the ocean's coastline and travel to the other coast, the West Coast of the United States. The prophecy went on to say something very important about the ones who would obey this message from the Lord. It stated, "Blessed will be the offspring of those who are in obedience, leaving their land and traveling to this new land America. They will be a blessing to the nations. God will pour blessings on them, and they will prosper and flourish."

A SECOND PROPHECY!

Shortly after this vision, the Boy Prophet gave a second prophecy about an event which would follow the first prophecy. This prophecy was placed in a securely sealed envelope to be opened by a person of the Lord's choosing and in His timing. God's warning to the Boy Prophet said if the second prophecy was not opened by the Lord's chosen one, the imposter would surely die. Many believe this second prophecy tells about a time when Christians would once again be forced to leave their homes because of a similarly dangerous situation.

I wondered, *what the danger was which would be coming in the future? When would the second prophecy be opened?* Of course, the other big question was; *who would open it?*

Both prophecies were faithfully protected and stored in a safe place, while the Armenians waited on God for a better understanding of what the Boy Prophet had written. They also waited for the Lord's timing on when they should leave. It was during this time that there was a great outpouring of the Holy Spirit. This beautiful outpouring flowed through Armenia, which had begun in Russia. My great-great-grandparents were among the first to receive this powerful anointing.

"Could I be a blessing to the nations?"

REFLECTING ON THESE POWERFUL WORDS

As my grandparents shared the incredible story of the Boy Prophet and the first prophecy he gave at age eleven, I thought about his words, "The offspring of those who obeyed will be a blessing to the nations." I knew I was part of that offspring and it connected me to this prophecy. I could not grasp the idea of fleeing to another land. I could not imagine the life my ancestors lived.

Hearing about Kara Kala, Armenia, and the nations, I felt they were far removed from me and my comfortable life in Southern California. And yet silently, inside this shy little eight-year-olds mind I asked the Lord, "Could I be a blessing to the nations? Could I be used? Was I born with purpose too!"

"Demos Shakarian massively and positively impacted the lives of many Nigerian business people across our great nation of Nigeria with proofs that cannot be denied. While a very large number of men and women came to know the Lord through his platform, many believers from Orthodox churches also experienced the baptism of the Holy Ghost. All the testimonies of transformed lives and business breakthroughs happened because of him.

Without any doubt, Demos Shakarian has left footprints on the sands of time in the body of Christ globally. To God be all the glory!"

— **David Oyedepo** • Bishop / Living Faith Church Worldwide, Nigeria
Winners' Chapel International / Chancellor, Covenant University

CHAPTER TWO

Goodbye Kara Kala

Whether as a child or as an adult, I never tired of hearing about our unique family history. Realistically I knew every family was unique, but my grandparents instilled in me a solid base upon which it was easy for me to understand and appreciate how everyone in my past played a part of who I am, and where I am today.

There were a few in my family who not only laid the foundation but represented the cornerstone upon which everything else was built. Their story and legacy of faith continue ...

My grandfather particularly loved retelling the events surrounding the birth of my great-grandfather Isaac, who was born in Kara Kala. Isaac's father was also named Demos. My grandfather never knew his grandfather Demos, but he would have a great influence on him. My grandfather was living in America directly because of his namesake.

Great-great-grandfather Demos had died many years before my grandfather was born. This was surprising as Bobby included such details in his storytelling that it was hard to believe he hadn't experienced these events first-hand.

Great-great-grandfather Demos had five daughters: Shushan, Esther, Siroon, Magga, and Yerchan. While he adored his daughters, having a son was much more of an honor in old

Armenia. Though I did not understand this completely, I had noticed boys appeared to be given preferential treatment over myself and my older sister Denice, by some of the old-world Armenians. I was thankful that I never felt a difference from my grandparents, being their *granddaughter*.

Around 1850, my great-great-grandfather Demos lived in Kara Kala. The majority of Armenians were people of devout faith, they were Russian Orthodox, but great-great-grandfather and many others in the town were Presbyterian. They viewed prophecy as something which happened only in the Old Testament.

My ancestors were first introduced to the Holy Spirit on a personal level, through a prophecy about the birth of Great-grandfather Isaac. The prophecy was spoken to Isaac's mother by her brother Magardich, who was visiting the family.

My great-great-grandparents and their five daughters lived in a one-room farmhouse, which is where all the girls were born. Though the family had little money, they would wake up on Sunday mornings and put on their best traditional clothing before walking into town to attend church, usually held in some-one's home. Despite his lack of resources and his desire to have a son, Great-great-grandfather Demos would walk ahead of his wife and children (as was customary) with his shoulders pulled back and a smile on his face.

Great-great-grandfather Demos was proud of his family. Even though he loved his wife and loved each of his daughters, he desperately wanted to have a son. He took great care to show his wife, his children and his town that he believed each of his daughters was a blessing. Grandfather always described this scene with such passion. I could feel myself walking behind Great-great-grandfather Demos down the dirt road and alongside my great-great-grandmother and their daughters.

Gathering at the house church was the highlight of the week. The service was conducted in Russian. Although Great-great-grandfather Demos understood Russian; he did not understand the full meaning of the Holy Spirit. Nor could he entirely grasp the lessons taught to the Russian Orthodox Christians.

> *He was praying for a miracle: that God would honor him with a son.*

Yet he had a desire and a need, so he stood in that small, crowded gathering every Sunday morning. Secretly, he was praying for a miracle: *that God would honor him with a son.*

GOOD OL' UNCLE MAGARDICH

Uncle Magardich was one of the first in our family to receive the Baptism of the Holy Spirit. He shared his experiences with his sister Goolisar, Great-great-grandfather Demos' wife, about this newfound joy.

One rainy day, May 25, 1891, to be exact, Magardich visited my great-great-grandmother Goolisar at her home. A few other ladies from Kara Kala were also visiting. On this day her brother could sense a deep sadness which had fallen over her. No matter what Magardich said, he was unable to lift her mood. Goolisar sat alone, barely participating with the rest of the guests. Though she was energetic by nature, Magardich suddenly felt that his sister had aged more so than her years could account for.

Magardich started reading his Bible and inquiring of the Lord about his sister when he suddenly looked up at her. "Goolisar!" he said. "I just heard from the Lord," he enthusiastically announced.

"It was about you!" "What did He say?" Goolisar asked with great caution, still not feeling hopeful. Magardich proclaimed, "The Lord told me He is going to give you a son exactly one year from today!"

Magardich spoke these words with authority. He did not question their authenticity. He had received a message from the Lord, and he knew it to be true. Goolisar, on the other hand, must have thought her brother was crazy! She had longed for a son for so long, and she wanted to believe that just maybe this was a Word from God. Though cautious upon hearing the prophecy, she chose to believe it came directly from the Lord.

Goolisar was excited to share the prophecy with her husband. She anxiously waited for him to return from working on the farm. When he walked through the door,

He made sure to have plenty of flowers and candles on hand to set the mood!

she revealed to him the news with tears filling her eyes. "Magardich was given a message from the Lord today," she told my great-great-grandfather. "The Lord said I would be given a son exactly one year from today!"

As Goolisar repeated these words to her husband, she felt great excitement. For so many years they both had waited and prayed for a son. A rush of emotions swept over her, and she began to weep. Her husband comforted her. Through her joy, she described the day to him. Great-great-grandfather Demos desperately wanted to believe her, but he was filled with doubts. He questioned the prophecy. *Is the Lord really speaking directly to Magardich? Could the Lord be answering my prayer,* he wondered? In secret hope and anticipation, Great-great-grandfather Demos decided to wait and see. And being a man, it's not inconceivable he made sure to have plenty of flowers and candles on hand to set the mood ... just to help the Lord along!

PROPHESY FULFILLED

A few months later, sure enough, Goolisar was expecting her sixth child!

By this time, word of Magardich's prophecy had spread through the village. Everyone in Kara Kala wondered whether Goolisar and Demos would finally have their son. The whole town was on pins and needles, but no one more than my great-great-grandfather. He did not want a possible sixth daughter to be greeted with disappointment but filled with excitement he wondered: *Will it be a boy? Wait and see.* Though he told himself privately, *It's a boy.*

His answer came on May 25, 1892, exactly one year from the day the prophecy was given to Uncle Magardich. Goolisar gave birth to a baby boy, *Isaac.* It was the perfect name for this child, "A son of promise." He was my great-grandfather, and his birth was prophesied just like in the Bible when Isaac's birth had also been prophesied. *The Biblical Isaac was born to Abraham when he was 100 years old and to Sarah, who was past 90.*

The whole town was thrilled hearing the news! I can imagine the sheer joy which filled the one-room farmhouse with the arrival of a baby boy. At last, after having five girls, God had blessed Demos and Goolisar with a son. This fulfilled the prophecy in every detail, including the date of his birth.

Isaac was not the last of Demos and Goolisar's children. When Isaac was four, Goolisar gave birth to another child, a daughter they named *Hamas.* Isaac's birth was a joyous introduction to the ways of the Spirit. The questions my great-great-grandfather once had about the Holy Spirit began to decrease because of the prophesied birth of baby Isaac.

My great-great-grandfather had no idea soon after this birth he would have an encounter with the Holy Spirit which would change his heart, his understanding, and his spiritual life forever. Though my grandfather never knew *his grandfather*, I was thankful I had known my great-grandfather, Isaac. In the same term of endearment in which I called my grandfather "Bobby," I lovingly referred to Great-grandfather Isaac as "Great-Bobby." This made hearing of my Great-Bobby's birth especially meaningful.

> *I lovingly referred to my great-grandfather Isaac as "Great-Bobby."*

THE STEER'S HEAD – A GODFATHER MOMENT

In 1900 when Isaac was eight years old, his father learned a huge group of Russian Christians was coming to Kara Kala. Tradition held everyone who came to visit would be well taken care of and especially well fed. So my great-great-grandfather Demos decided to honor the Russian Christians and host a celebratory feast.

The whole town worked together to prepare for the arrival of their honored guests. Great-great-grandfather Demos took great care of the cattle he raised and chose the best from his small herd for the feast. In my eight-year-old mind, the steer was shiny and black, 1,200 pounds of fury with ferocious white horns atop its head!

But as it came to be, Great-great-grandfather noticed the steer had one blind eye. Though this would not compromise the taste of the meat, he believed he should not choose an imperfect animal for this feast. He knew his Bible scriptures and heavily considered Leviticus 22:20 which reads, "Do not present an animal with defects, because the Lord will not accept it on your behalf." After all, many would be arriving from the neighboring churches, including the Priest!

The problem was, no other steer was big enough to feed all the guests, and he could not afford to kill two of his animals. Contemplating the decision for some time and against his better judgment, he finally decided to kill the big steer and prepare it for the celebration. He then felt remorse for his decision, so he decided to hide the head of the flawed steer in the corner of his barn.

He hurriedly dug a shallow hole making sure no one was watching, bagged the steer's head and placed it inside the hole. He covered it with dirt and put a shovel and a few other farm tools on top.

As I remember hearing this crazy story from Grandfather, I imagined it as a scene straight out of "The Godfather." Music swelling with anticipation in the background as the bloodied steer's head is buried so no one could ever find it. I envisioned Marlon Brando or Al Pacino entering the story at any moment!

I imagined it as a scene straight out of "The Godfather."

As Great-great-grandfather Demos finished preparing the animal for the celebration, he heard the sound of approaching covered wagons. The leader of the group of Russian Christians was an older man with a white beard, who dressed elegantly and sat higher than the rest of the attendants. He was clearly recognized as the patriarch, prophet, and priest. My great-great-grandfather, with his cherished son Isaac running closely behind him rushed to welcome their special guests.

THE CELEBRATORY FEAST

Every family in the town was preparing food for the celebration. As the sun set and the evening began to fall, the townspeople gathered in front of my great-great-grandparents' home bringing whatever they had prepared for the meal. Excited and hungry, everyone found a place to sit. It was a very festive mood!

Before the feast could begin, the tradition was the food must be blessed. However, the Russians did not bless their food in the same way my ancestors did. The Russians did not pray until they felt the Lord's presence. In silence, they waited until they felt the Holy Spirit fall on them. Then, they would lift their arms and praise the Lord while dancing and singing, which was a sign they felt the Lord's presence was there.

My great-great-grandfather was not confident in his relationship with the Holy Spirit at this point. Though he had been blessed with his son through prophecy, he still wasn't quite sure about the whole thing. Certainly, he did not feel comfortable joining in.

The Russian Christians, on the other hand, were *sure* of their faith. They waited for the anointing of the Holy Spirit to fall upon them. The townspeople watched as slowly but surely, one Russian Christian after another began to rejoice and praise the Lord.

Great-great-grandfather assumed after this display of worship the blessing of the food would come next. He was unprepared for what happened instead!

The festivities had turned quite loud. Some of the townspeople had brought instruments they were playing. Many were laughing and enjoying the evening when the white-bearded

Russian patriarch suddenly raised his hand to stop the festivities. A silence fell upon the crowd as the Russians, and the
townspeople from Kara Kala fixed their eyes upon him. With
his eyes glued to my great-great-grandfather, the patriarch
stood and walked away from the crowd, and went right past my
great-great-grandparents' house. Great-great-grandfather realized
with astonished disbelief; he was heading straight for the barn!

Oh Great-great-grandfather Demos, what a mess! Beads of
sweat began to form on his forehead. Though he felt confident he
had hidden the steer's head, he felt ashamed. *Calm down,* Great-
great-grandfather said to himself, *you have hidden the evidence in
the deepest, darkest, most remote part of the barn. The Russian priest
could not possibly find the steer's head. Or could he?*

Moments later, the white-bearded priest emerged from
the barn and much to my great-great-grandfather's complete
shock; he was carrying the steer's bagged head in his hand. My
great-great-grandfather began to tremble as the priest approached
him. He kept thinking, *how could he have known about the steer's
head buried in the barn?* After all, he was sure no one had seen him
hide the bag!

Without saying a word, the priest walked solemnly until he
was standing right in front of Great-great-grandfather. In dramatic silence, the priest dropped the bag from which the head
of the steer with the blind eye was displayed for all to see. In
what sounded like a collective rumbling, the guests of the grand
celebration gasped!

His voice booming, the Russian priest finally addressed my
great-great-grandfather.

"Do you have something to tell us?" he shouted. Great-great-
grandfather was mortified. With a shaky voice, he responded,

"Yes." His usually strong shoulders slumped, as he looked toward the ground and the bloodied steer's head. Then he lifted his head. Curiosity set upon him. "How did you know?" he asked the Russian priest. "Did someone tell you? No one saw me!"

At that moment, any shame he felt was lifted, and Great-great-grandfather was filled with a surprising feeling. As the townspeople watched this cover-up unfold, Great-great-grandfather Demos felt enveloped in love and warmth. "God told me," said the priest. Though still commanding, his voice was now softer and comforting. "You know that God speaks to His children today. The Holy Spirit told me about the steer's head because he wanted you to believe in His power. You have questioned the outpouring of the Holy Spirit, but you will not oppose the Holy Spirit anymore. In fact, starting today, you will welcome the Holy Spirit into your life completely."

"Tell me how I can receive the Spirit of God. I want to receive Him."

Upon hearing these powerful words, tears began streaming down my great-great-grandfather's sun-weathered face. Standing there in front of everyone, he began repenting. He asked not only for forgiveness from the Russian Christians and the Lord but also from all of his guests. He said, "Tell me how I can receive the Spirit of God. I want to receive Him."

In the words of my grandfather, *his* grandfather knelt down before the tall Russian priest as he laid his hands on Great-great-grandfather's head. As soon as he did, Great-great-grandfather Demos began to offer a joyful prayer in a language he could not understand. He was told this prayerful expression was called "speaking in tongues." It was a sign the Holy Spirit was speaking through him in a prayerful language.

That night was more than a celebration of Great-great-grandfather Demos' welcoming of the Holy Spirit. Later that evening, Goolisar also received the prayerful language. It turned out to be a very important night, as the lives of my great-great-grandparents were transformed forever!

> "We will never forget walking into one of Demos' meetings, as young ministers in the early eighties. Fear and trepidation tried to grip us as we walked through the doors, thinking there would be a religious and judgmental atmosphere. But Demos Shakarian had created such a warm group of businessmen who walked in the love of God. It didn't matter if we were just barely thirty. The wisdom and joy permeated those meetings and changed my heart that very day."
>
> **— Mary Hudson** • Arise Conferences

GOODBYE, KARA KALA

By 1900, the Boy Prophet's vision was forty-seven years old. Almost five decades passed since Efim Gerasemovitch Klubniken had prophesied about a future disaster when they were to flee from Armenia to the west coast of America. Efim was now 58 years-old when he announced, "The prophecy soon will be fulfilled." It was time to leave the country. The moment so many Armenians were waiting for was here!

My great-great-grandparents eventually also heeded the warning, as the unrest in Kara Kala was increasingly growing. It was no longer safe to worship the Lord openly or in their beloved home churches as they had done for decades. Now they had to meet secretly out in fields to worship God together.

The Boy Prophet was the first to leave Kara Kala and do exactly what the prophecy said. He did not hesitate when God said it was time to go and did as he was directed nearly five decades earlier. Others followed, and slowly a great number of Armenians left Kara Kala and the nearby towns; in pursuit of the new land God had shown the Boy Prophet at the age of eleven.

They knew there was something significant they must bring with them. The second written prophecy! So it was painstakingly preserved and brought to America. It was carefully stored away in Los Angeles, waiting once again to hear from the Lord as to *when* the second prophecy should be opened and read. And of course, *by whom?*

Among those who fled were my great-great-grandparents. Though the farm had been in the family for generations in Armenia, they sold their possessions for whatever they could get and fled as God had instructed them to do.

My grandparents explained, when the Boy Prophet had initially written the prophetic warning in Russian; my great-great-grandfather *was* skeptical. However, years later after Isaac's prophesied birth and his experience with the Russian priest, my great-great-grandparents never questioned the operation of the Holy Spirit again. They knew He was real and operating today just as in the days of old.

"Mr. Demos Shakarian's family walked in the supernatural through the guidance of the Holy Spirit, walking in the Spirit in Armenia and not after the flesh. They would obey God in the gravest hour of their life and strengthened by that Word; they moved out of their comfort zone to America in faith. They left behind everything as Abraham did. His obedience protected his family's life and their spiritual grace, which was their divine calling to increase and bless the world. This obedience ignited the revelations about the cattle, to the reaching of the businessmen around the world for Christ.

This Era Shall Begin Again Once This Book Is Released! The anointed young people shall see visions to prepare the world for His coming.

I had the great opportunity to meet and hear Mr. Demos in Singapore in the 1980's. His passion was to win souls and to establish His Kingdom. During the altar calls, he would personally go down to the altars and lead people to Christ and pray with them. God's love in him overflowed, which transformed the speakers and their audience to also flow in love.

He never tired of testifying of God's power. He gave many hope! Every servant of God would go out of his Convention with the strength of the Holy Spirit determined to do great things for God. Thanks to the seed planted by Demos Shakarian, I was encouraged to grow our ministry in India. I salute this great 'General of the Holy Spirit.' By faith, Demos Shakarian's vision continues to increase.

'A righteous man will be remembered forever' Psalms 112: 6."

— Paul Dhinakaran, Ph.D. • President / Jesus Calls International, Chancellor / Karunya University, India

CHAPTER THREE

California Here We Come!

❦

I remember hurriedly getting ready to go with my Bobby to the car wash. I put on my favorite bright-yellow pinafore dress with my white patent leather Mary-Jane shoes. I wanted to look so pretty for my Bobby. Before leaving my bedroom, I glanced in the mirror one more time to make sure everything was perfect, and noticed my right frilly-white sock had fallen down. So I quickly fixed it. Now I was perfect, and then I ran out of the room. What would you expect from a 10-year-old girl?

I just knew the car wash was *the place* to be. It seemed to be where everyone would meet and catch up with one another. What a treat it was, going to the car wash with my Bobby. As I would swing my little legs back and forth on the beach-like chairs, being careful not to sit on my long hair, I watched as people came and went. As the customers walked by, they seemed to gravitate to Grandfather. Gradually, people would come over to speak with him. I was extremely timid, and I noticed how easily my Bobby could make conversation, even with those he didn't know. Talking to everyone seemed easy for him, but I found out much later speaking to crowds did not come naturally.

Going to the Downey Car Wash appeared to be not only a delight for me, but also for Grandfather. He introduced me to everyone and I felt he was as proud of me, as I was of him. "This is my beautiful granddaughter, Cynthia," he would tell people before boasting about my latest hobby or achievement. Feeling embarrassed while playing with my hair, he helped me to be more confident after spending time with him. Like I could do anything I set my mind too!

Bobby would tell me another adventure as we sat and watched the attendants drying the cars. He was never in a hurry when spending time together. He treated me as if he had all the time in the world, like nothing was more important to him. His attitude and the love he showed made me feel incredibly special.

HEEDING THE PROPHETIC WARNING

The Boy Prophet and his family left Armenia approximately five years after the feast with the Russian Christians. My great-great-grandparents and their family left some time later. Many in Armenia *did not* believe *the Prophecy* and ridiculed the Armenians who had regarded it as a warning from the Lord. Some mocked the "prophecy believing Christians," as the mass exodus began.

The year was around 1905 when my family left their home, the only one they had ever known. The Armenians continued their departure and migration to the United States until around 1912, when the majority of people who were planning on leaving, had now fled.

My great-great-grandparents left most of their belongings behind. They took only the personal possessions their nine-person family could carry. My great-great-grandparents, their five eldest daughters (Shushan, Esther, Siroon, Magga, and Yerchan), their treasured son (Isaac 13 years-old) and their youngest daughter (Hamas 9 years-old), said goodbye to Kara Kala. Years later, Hamas Shakarian would marry a man named Tom Kardashian. Hamas and Tom's son, Arthur, was the father of Robert Kardashian, the attorney who gained national recognition as O.J. Simpson's attorney.

As an adult, I knew Robert to be a very genuine, extremely kind and a loyal man. He deeply loved and cherished his four beautiful children. In fact, in most conversations, he usually would mention a recent achievement of one of them. Some of my favorite memories of him were eating at Robert's favorite Armenian restaurant "Carousel" with family members. Most importantly, I knew him to be a man who loved the Lord. He is greatly loved and enormously missed!

> "Demos and Rose were two of the sweetest and most embracing people I ever knew. I'm related through my grandma who was Demos' Auntie, through his Dad Isaac's youngest sister, Hamas. I recall growing up as cousins with Geri (Demos and Rose's daughter) and Cheryl Babajian. We had sleepovers on occasion, and they would visit me on Balboa Island in Newport Beach when we spent summers there.
>
> As a young girl attending my grandparents' church (Hamas Shakarian Kardashian and Tom Kardashian), I recall Rose playing the piano. She could REALLY play that gospel music, with the chords running up and down the keys in every direction! I loved watching her from my perch next to my grandma's knee. Of course (as is Armenian tradition) the women and men were segregated. Fortunately, the piano was located close to where I was sitting, and I was able to see Rose's fingers fly. She was an inspiration.

Now I realize she was not only gifted musically, but filled with the Holy Spirit who made her music supernaturally wonderful.

Demos was my Dad's first cousin and greatly resembled him. I thought they looked so much alike and he was always especially loved and respected by me for this reason. It was also because they both had such loving temperaments. Of course, his kindness overflowed, but so did his Dad's — my great uncle, Isaac.

Their testimony and family history filled in chunks of my grandma's history. It also explains my heritage. This has given me a tremendous respect for what the Lord has done in guiding our families. We cling to the witness!"

— **Barbara Kardashian Carr** • Granddaughter of my great-grandfather Isaac's youngest sister, Hamas / Demos' second-cousin / Sister of Robert Kardashian

THE PROMISE

As they set out for the new land, Great-great-grandfather Demos, Goolisar and their children; clung to the promise that "God would bless and prosper them, and cause their seed to be a blessing to the nations." I am sure they could never have imagined the magnitude of how the prophecy of blessing would be fulfilled through their heirs, in particular through the life of Grandfather Demos.

Many other people from Kara Kala and the surrounding towns also chose to leave—one family and then another, with many settling in California. My great-great-grandparents were faced with a horrible situation. They left their farm, which had been passed down for generations. They left their livestock, which was their livelihood and financial security.

They left their house, many of their possessions and friends in the familiar setting of Kara Kala, to travel to a new land far away from their beloved Armenia.

They had little or no idea of where they were going except to follow the roughly sketched map of the Boy Prophet. They didn't know what they would find when they arrived. They did not know the language, the culture or the topography. They knew only one thing: *that God had given them a mandate, and they must go!*

DESTRUCTION BEGINS IN ARMENIA

The year 1915, brought terrible times to the Armenians who chose to stay. Though, I have heard about the heroics of some loving and compassionate people as well. I believe it is important to also tell the stories of the heroes — the people who helped others during this abhorrent time in history and lead some Armenians to safety.

I believe it is important to also tell the stories of the heroes.

A dear friend relayed to me about her Armenian grandfather Bedros, who was a young boy when the rebels began attacking Armenians. The band of rebels did unspeakable things to those living there at the time. However, Bedros had a wonderful Turkish friend. They had grown up together and loved one another like brothers. When the rebels came to Bedros's village, all hell broke loose, and people ran for their lives!

Yet, the Turkish friend and his family protected Bedros. Risking their lives, they hid him under a bed as the rebel soldiers went from house to house looking for Armenians. Their love for Bedros was stronger than the fear they felt in the face of such danger, and their act of kindness saved his life. Later the family helped sneak her grandfather out of Armenia. The two boys came to America together and remained great friends in this new land.

The Turkish boy, now a man, was always referred to as Mr. Kelley. After coming to America, God blessed him in many ways. He became extremely successful. He was also loved by all, especially by my friend's grateful family for his selfless act in protecting their grandfather as a boy. After her grandfather Bedros died, her father continued to take their family to Florida every Easter so they could visit Mr. Kelley. The family kept this tradition honoring him for saving their grandfather's life until Mr. Kelly passed away.

Now that I am aware of this heroic story of compassion, someone who risked his life to keep his friend safe from harm, I also honor the memory of Mr. Kelly.

Unfortunately, not all Armenians who remained experienced the same outcome as Bedros or my ancestors who left Armenia and were safe in America. By the end of the Armenian Genocide, somewhere between eight-hundred-thousand and 1.5 million Armenians had been massacred by rebels. Some reports have the number of lives lost as much greater. Sadly, this included many of the people who had ridiculed the Christian Armenians for believing the Prophesy.

Many of those who remained in Armenia were given a choice to denounce Christ or perish. As the prophecy had warned, many who did not flee according to the prophetic warning lost their lives, choosing death over the denial of their Lord and Savior.

"I was raised as an Armenian Orthodox Christian in Jerusalem, occasionally attending services at the beautiful 12th-century church, that is the heart of the Armenian Quarter in the Old City of Jerusalem. Growing up, I didn't realize I could have a relationship with God and never even considered I should read the Bible on my own. When I began my journey of faith in my early 20's, I started reading the Bible from the beginning but shortly after gave up. Then I read Demos Shakarian's life story. I happily delved in because I knew anyone with the name Shakarian was Armenian and therefore had automatic credibility with me. To this day, I am grateful because Demos marked a pivotal point in my life — launching my personal relationship with God.

Throughout his journey, I saw how God orchestrated and ordained every step which Demos took. His life showed me God exists and His miracles are as real today as they were in the days of old. I never met Demos Shakarian, but his influence in my life was transformational. He was indeed a giant of faith, a man who heard, followed and trusted God with every fiber of his being."

— **Tony Jansezian** • Fellow Armenian from Jerusalem, Israel

ARRIVING IN NEW YORK

When Great-great-grandfather Demos and his family had traveled over fifty-six-hundred miles, they finally arrived in New York, knowing the first part of their journey was complete. Yet, the details recorded in the prophecy were specific, telling them not to stop until they arrived on the West Coast, almost another three-thousand miles away.

Many of the families from Kara Kala were with them on their quest to reach the West Coast. My great-great-grandfather along with his wife, six daughters and beloved son Isaac, continued to make their way across this new country. They were thrilled when finally arriving in Los Angeles, California. Soon they were reunited with other Armenians who settled there. Great-great-grandfather found a place to live with their help. He and his family were now able to begin their new life in America!

The first home my great-great-grandfather Demos, Goolisar, and their seven children lived in was located at 919 Boston Street, which was in one of the least expensive areas the family could find. There were so many people from their village in the same area; they nicknamed their neighborhood "little Kara Kala."

> They nicknamed their neighborhood "little Kara Kala."

I can still close my eyes and see it in my imagination, based solely on the description my grandfather gave me. This area is now known as Boyle Heights.

The home was basically a roof over their heads and a safe haven for my family. There was nothing special about it—far from it. Yet I imagined this home was filled with love, possibly because the family infused it with such warmth.

Through the eyes of a child, this seemed like a fun adventure. As I have grown older, I see the situation through the eyes of an adult. With limited funds and in desperate need of a place for his family, my great-great-grandfather was able to move into the home only by joining with two other families who had also just arrived from Armenia. Though the way my Bobby talked about the house made me think of it as a special place. My great-great-grandfather was continually grateful to the Lord for the home and for guiding them safely to America.

Because of this and his love for the Lord, Great-great-grandfather Demos openly knelt down to pray each day. As he fell to his knees in prayer, his son Isaac looked on. This made a lasting impression on him. Great-grandfather Isaac passed this same gratitude down to my grandfather Demos.

LOOKING FOR WORK

After settling in Los Angeles, the next challenge my great-great-grandfather faced was to find a job so he could provide for his family. Each morning, he would walk down an area very similar to today's day-labor sites. Day after day, he would leave early in the morning in hopes of finding a job, only to return in the evening without success.

> *Great-great-grandfather Demos openly knelt down to pray each day.*

I realize now what a difficult life my ancestors had lived. Though Great-great-grandfather Demos and Goolisar were far from wealthy, when living in Armenia they were comfortable, and all their needs were met. Plus Great-great-grandfather was raising cattle on his farm, which is what he loved to do!

In this new land, that was not the case. He was concerned how he would feed his wife and seven children. More than ever, I see how they struggled to provide for their family and build a whole new life in this unfamiliar land. Now I understand the full meaning of my grandfather's words and the emotion he felt when he talked about *his grandfather Demos.*

Hard work was a regular part of life. People did what was necessary to make it through the day. Working hard is part of the Armenian culture. The optimism though, now that was something different. Their optimism was given to them by their trust in God and the Boy Prophet's words, who had spoken of a coming time of abundance and blessings. Armenians who had fled to the West Coast clung to "the Promise" of a future which would bless their descendants.

Working hard throughout the week, my great-great-grandparents and their community of Armenian immigrants looked forward to the bright spot which ended each week. That day was Sunday, a day when they held a Sunday service in their new home, just like the house churches back in Kara Kala. Many of the Armenians and Russians who had fled came to my great-great-grandparents home, as it quickly became known as the center of worship.

With an open Bible lying prominently and placed for all to see.

The house at 919 Boston Street had a large living room which converted into a meeting place. The format for the service was also reflective of the house churches, with an open Bible lying prominently and placed for all to see. The men sat on one side of the room, and the women sat on the other. On Sundays, everyone dressed in their traditional Armenian garments, which they brought from the old country.

The churchgoers kept an important Armenian tradition in place. When someone had a need or a special request, that person would kneel before the Bible waiting to hear from the Lord. Everyone else would begin to pray. Being led by the Spirit, someone would approach the open Bible and seek an answer from God for this person.

Regardless of the situation, everyone was encouraged by the Scripture they received in answer to their individual request or need.

AZUSA STREET

Something amazing happened one day as my great-great-grandfather and his brother-in-law, good ol' Uncle Magardich Mushegan, searched for work at the local horse stables. As they walked down the streets of Los Angeles passing Azusa Street, a sound penetrated through all the noise of this busy street where day-laborers gathered to find work. The sound was so powerful it stopped them in their tracks. It was something they had heard before in Armenia. It was the beautiful sound of people praising and worshiping God by speaking in tongues. It was a miracle! They had no knowledge of anyone in this new nation who worshiped as they did back in Armenia, praising God in the Spirit!

Great-great-grandfather Demos and Magardich hurried toward the sound, discovering it was coming from a converted stable. They timidly peeked in. Suddenly the door was thrown open, and they were surrounded by worshippers who welcomed them without reservation. The two brothers-in-law lifted their hands and thanked God for this amazing discovery.

It became known as the famous "Azusa Street Revival."

Later, Great-great-grandfather and Magardich said goodbye to their new friends on Azusa Street and headed back home. They returned to their families with exciting news to share about their friends in the converted horse stable. With their families, they celebrated the discovery of this beautiful presence on Azusa Street and saw it as a sign from God.

This area would become known as the famous "Azusa Street Revival." It was here, the power of God became real to a huge cross-section of races and religions. This experience marked for my family and many others, the kindling of an even larger out-pouring of the Holy Spirit which would spread around the world.

HEADING FOR NEVADA

Every day Great-great-grandfather left early in search of work. This went on for some time with no success. One day he returned home, and his family immediately recognized the change in his countenance. Excitedly, he called the family together to share his good news. California's Great Depression had impacted his ability to find work, but he had finally found a job.

The problem was the job was in Nevada, where the railroads were hiring men. Great-great-grandfather Demos was so excited. He felt he would finally be able to provide for his family. His family however, was extremely concerned—particularly Goolisar. As he told his wife the details of the job, she became increasingly upset. She had heard about the hot desert climate which sometimes reached unbearable temperatures. Other families had told her about men who had dropped dead in the extreme heat while laying railroad tracks.

My great-great-grandfather tried to ease his family's concerns reminding them as a farmer he was accustomed to working outside in the sun. Moreover, this seemed to be the only job available. According to their custom, he called all the attendants of their house-church together to pray for his new job and bless him, before he left to start work almost 300 miles away. Leaving with only an extra pair of pants and shirt, he said goodbye to his wife and children, hugging them tightly, and headed for the deserts of Nevada to work on the railroad.

My great-great-grandfather sent home his paycheck at

the end of every week, which continued for about a year. One evening Goolisar received a wire with devastating news confirming the worst of her fears. My great-great-grandfather Demos had collapsed suddenly and died while working on the rail-line due to extremely high temperatures. His body would be transported back to Los Angeles by train.

After fleeing from Armenia and coming all the way to California, his life was taken soon upon arriving. He never lived to see the blessings of the seed the Boy Prophet had described. That seed would start with Great-grandfather Isaac and eventually Isaac's son, my grandfather Demos!

> "Demos Shakarian believed God's power could impact and transform every person in society, as it is not limited to an expression within the four walls of the church or an account in the Bible. When he realized men were not attending the Tent meetings and churches in Southern California nearly as much as women were, he founded his organization to attract men towards a supernatural encounter with God.
>
> Indeed, our society is filled with the sad tales of broken homes and a fatherless generation. I believe Demos' mission to reach out to men was and is of vital importance. The Apostle Paul said he sought to be all things to all people that he might, by all means, save some. (1 Corinthians 9:22)
>
> Shakarian, like the Apostle Paul, was willing to use a different angle—business—to reach people for Jesus. This is the heart of God.
>
> I consider Demos Shakarian a pioneer in his day. His legacy continues to be an inspiration."
>
> **— Guillermo Maldonado** • Apostle / King Jesus
> International Ministry

CHAPTER FOUR

Head of the House
at Fourteen

❧

I was much taller than my girlfriends at 13 years-old, and my platform shoes only exaggerated my height. I can remember wearing one of my favorite pants; bright royal-blue tightly fitting bell-bottoms and a matching velvet-ribbon choker necklace. I know you might be thinking, *that must have looked quite funny.* But as a brand new teenager, I thought I was really stylin! My grandfather commented on how pretty his "Cynthia jan" was, but I know he had to have been chuckling under his breath because my outfit was a bit out there!

My grandfather had taken me to one of his favorite local restaurants, Foxys. Seated near the entrance, we felt the cold February wind blow in each time a patron entered or left the restaurant. I can remember the scene: My grandfather and I, sitting in a booth deep in conversation as though no one else was around and nothing else mattered to me at that moment. He had my full attention!

My grandfather enjoyed talking about *his father,* Isaac, and *his grandfather,* Demos, but this time felt different. I clung to my Bobby's every word as a tear began rolling down his round cheek. As I looked into his eyes, I said, "Bobby, are you crying?"

He proceeded to share how *his grandfather* left this earth while trying to provide for his family. "It would have meant so much to me to have met my grandfather," he said under his breath. It gave him great peace knowing he would be able to spend time with him in Heaven. I felt great compassion when my grandfather told me what happened in the days, months, and years after his grandfather's passing from this earth.

As the conversation continued, I scooted closer to my Bobby wiping his tear with my hand. He looked at me, and a big smile came across his face as he continued the story. He was so proud of how his father Isaac handled the tragic event of losing his father at such a young age.

When my great-great-grandfather went to Heaven, Isaac was 14 years-old. With the passing of his father, Isaac became the man of the house. Though Isaac was just a boy, Armenian tradition dictated, the oldest male in the family became responsible for everyone in his home. It did not matter that Isaac had five older sisters, one younger sister, and a mother. At fourteen years old he was now responsible for caring and financially providing for his entire family!

EXTRA, EXTRA . . . READ ALL ABOUT IT

Isaac found himself selling newspapers on a street corner in downtown Los Angeles, earning about $10.00 per month. It may not sound like much money, but in 1906, Isaac's monthly contribution to the family household made a big difference.

However, Isaac's newspaper income was not enough to support the entire family. In keeping with "old-world" Armenian traditions, he refused to allow his mother to get a job. Instead, he began looking for work all over town following in his father's footsteps. Jobs were hard to find, and a boy of Isaac's age had even less potential to find work. He finally found a job in a harness factory. It paid slightly better than selling newspapers. Though, his income was still not enough to support his family. On top of that, the working conditions were terrible. Isaac developed a chronic cough from all the dust at the factory, which only worsened with time. The family doctor said, *if he did not stop working at the harness factory he might not live to see his twentieth birthday.*

Isaac knew he needed to make a change. Who else could support his family? Surely his new responsibilities as the man of the household seemed like a huge load to carry. Isaac must have felt overwhelmed with his new position, but was ready to do whatever it took to fulfill his duties. He was always thinking about how to bring in more money. He was determined to be the sole provider for his family and was confident he could do it. That was the Armenian way!

In an attempt to help her young son, Isaac's mother wanted to bring in extra money for the family by going to work. Though she appreciated her young son's love for his family, she didn't want him to take on the full burden of supporting everyone by himself. But Isaac wouldn't hear of it! He let his mother know how strongly he felt. It was his sole responsibility to be the provider. This included all of his family. He continued by saying, "The day you get a job Mother will be the day I move out of the family house. It will be clear you do not need my help anymore."

It would become very apparent how strongly Isaac felt about keeping the Armenian tradition. One day he came home, and his mother was not there. Isaac asked his sisters where she was.

Trying to soften the blow they explained, because he was so young she wanted to help pay some of the expenses. Finally, they confessed she had accepted work doing some washing and ironing for another family.

Isaac was saddened to know his mother had taken a job. More than being the son, more than being the man of the house, he felt he was betraying the Armenian way. Isaac shook his head as he walked into his bedroom. Finding a box, he began to pack all his belongings. As he set the box on the front porch waiting for his mother to return home, he began to question himself. *Did I fail my mom? Did I fail my family?*

Walking up towards the house, his mother saw Isaac waiting for her. Looking at the box filled with clothes, she knew he was leaving. She anxiously asked, "Where are you going, son?" Isaac replied, "Mom, I feel I have failed you and I am an embarrassment to you, and the family, and the Armenian way."

His sisters could be seen pulling the curtains back and peering through the windowsill, watching and waiting to see what Isaac was going to do next. With tears streaming down his mom's face, she vowed not to return to her new job if he promised not to leave. Isaac agreed and wrapped his arms around his mother hugging her in a long embrace, gently wiping her tears with a handkerchief. His sisters could see how much he adored his mother. Picking up the box filled with his belongings, he walked his mother into the house.

That evening around the dinner table everyone was grateful there were no empty chairs, but no one more so than Isaac. As the night wore on, one by one they bid good-night. Isaac preparing for bed continued to plan what he needed to do to get a better paying job, with better working conditions. Remembering what his Dad had taught him and how the Lord guided the family to safety in America, he decided to ask God for help.

DIVINE DIRECTION

The Armenian believers who once met in the large front room of my great-great-grandparents' home, had built a church building where they gathered each Sunday. It was a small structure with simple wood benches, where the men sat on one side of the room and the women on the other. Once again, a table with a large open Bible was placed prominently in the front of the church. As always the Bible was the central focus in any room it was placed.

The following Sunday Isaac approached the pedestal holding the open Bible, as he had seen his father do so many times. Kneeling in front of the table, he stated his need for a better paying job. A few elders, including *good-ol' Magardich and his son*, stood behind Isaac. As was customary, the elders waited until one of them was led to step forward and place a finger on the open Bible. This indicated the Lord's answer to Isaac's request.

He placed his finger on these verses and read aloud from Deuteronomy 28:1-14

On that day *Uncle Magardich's son*, Aram, was the one to step forward. He placed his finger on these verses and read aloud from Deuteronomy 28:1-14.

¹ *If you fully obey the Lord your God and carefully follow all his commands I give you today, the Lord your God will set you high above all the nations on earth.* ² *All these blessings will come on you and accompany you if you obey the Lord your God:*

³ *You will be blessed in the city and blessed in the country.*

⁴ The fruit of your womb will be blessed, and the crops of your land and the young of your livestock—the calves of your herds and the lambs of your flocks.

⁵ Your basket and your kneading trough will be blessed.

⁶ You will be blessed when you come in and blessed when you go out.

⁷ The Lord will grant that the enemies who rise up against you will be defeated before you. They will come at you from one direction but flee from you in seven.

⁸ The Lord will send a blessing on your barns and on everything you put your hand to. The Lord your God will bless you in the land he is giving you.

⁹ The Lord will establish you as his holy people, as he promised you on oath, if you keep the commands of the Lord your God and walk in obedience to him. ¹⁰ Then all the peoples on earth will see that you are called by the name of the Lord, and they will fear you. ¹¹ The Lord will grant you abundant prosperity—in the fruit of your womb, the young of your livestock and the crops of your ground—in the land he swore to your ancestors to give you.

¹² The Lord will open the heavens, the storehouse of his bounty, to send rain on your land in season and to bless all the work of your hands. You will lend to many nations but will borrow from none. ¹³ The Lord will make you the head, not the tail. If you pay attention to the commands of the Lord your God that I give you this day and carefully follow them, you will always be at the top, never at the bottom. ¹⁴ Do not turn aside from any of the commands I give you today, to the right or to the left, following other gods and serving them.

Though Grandfather loved the entire Bible, these scriptures, given to his father Isaac, were forever his favorite Bible verses.

They would go on to carry the family through one of the most difficult times they ever experienced.

This Scripture confirmed what was in Isaac's heart. Every day at the harness factory Isaac dreamed of farming, raising cattle and being outside like his father had done in Armenia. With his heart filled with faith, Isaac quit his job.

Isaac once again walked the streets of downtown Los Angeles in search of work. He was eager to relieve his family's financial stress and find better working conditions. Though Isaac never gave up on his dream to become a dairy farmer.

Passing fruit and vegetable stands, he wanted to purchase some for his family but noticed the local produce wasn't fresh and far too expensive. He thought, *What would happen if I could offer better produce at a better price to the people in Los Angeles?*

A HORSE NAMED JACK

With God's promise and this inspiration, Isaac began a produce business. It was truly a leap of faith as he had little money. Though, he *did* have an intuitive sense for business. Isaac took his small savings along with the dowry he saved for his sisters, and he bought a wagon and a horse, he named *Jack*.

Isaac did not waste time. Every morning he woke up early, hitched Jack to the wagon and headed for Downey. Downey is a suburb of Los Angeles about 15-miles away from his home. The horse-and-cart trip took several hours each day, but the long trip was worth it. Downey had the best produce, and Armenians owned many of the farms. He would purchase produce, load his wagon and make the three-hour journey back, toward town to sell his produce house to house.

As Isaac enjoyed the fresh, clean country air, he remembered his struggle to breathe while working at the harness factory. As he spent his days in the countryside, his health began to improve. Soon, Isaac's cough was gone. Returning to Los Angeles from Downey, Isaac would shout from his wagon about the produce he had for sale. He called out every fruit and vegetable available that day, "Freshly picked vegetables," he proudly exclaimed! "Juicy plums! Tree ripened Oranges! Cabbage and carrots right from the farm!"

The fruits and vegetables were fresh, and the prices were much lower. Isaac soon became known for his premium produce. He offered a great product at a fair price. This endeared him to the community and solidified his good reputation. By the time Isaac reached twenty years of age, he had a stable business. He was making great money, but something was missing.

Though he cherished his time with his beloved horse Jack, his thoughts began to wonder about another kind of companion. One with two legs instead of four!

ISAAC IS IN LOVE

In particular, Isaac's heart was set on a fifteen-year-old young lady, named Zarouhi Yessayian. He noticed that she was incredibly beautiful. During church, Isaac saw Zarouhi sneaking glances at him too! Her face would turn a deep shade of red when their eyes locked, only to nervously turn away. She found him interestingly handsome.

Yet, protocol prevented him from speaking with her until the families had given the blessing for the marriage to take place. Yes, that's right, *the marriage*! Courtship was not permitted. The head of both families needed to give permission. With Isaac's financial problems resolved and his ability to continue providing for his mother and sisters, he decided to ask permission to make Zarouhi his wife.

In the absence of his deceased father, Great-grandfather Isaac turned to a church leader he could trust. Stepping in for Isaac's father, the church leader visited Zarouhi's family to make the formal request for her hand in marriage. He reminded her parents of Isaac's great dedication to his family, the tremendous responsibility he shouldered when his father went to Heaven and his hard work ethic. He also told her parents that Isaac dreamed of saving enough money to start a dairy farm one day. Zarouhi's father granted his permission, and they were married a short time later.

I can only imagine their wedding day. The wedding was attended by many of the families who fled Armenia for Los Angeles. I'm sure many of his loyal customers from his produce business were also there to celebrate. Isaac must have been so proud to have all six of his sisters in attendance, including his little sister, Hamas. Proudly walking his mother down the aisle, he gave her a gentle kiss on the cheek and a tender embrace before seating her. As you can tell from how I describe this event, I'm a bit of a romantic. Isaac requested the Bible verses Deuteronomy 28:1-14 to be prayed over him and his bride. As the verses were read, his mother was flooded with joy watching her handsome and cherished son say his vows. She was remembering the day she married her beloved husband so many years ago in Armenia. Oh! How she longed for him, especially on this special day.

After their marriage, it wasn't long before Great-grandparents Isaac and Zarouhi saved enough to buy ten acres of land in Downey. Soon they purchased three cows as they worked towards Great-grandfather Isaac's dream of owning a dairy farm!

Isaac and his wife constructed their first home together as best they could, as it was not their expertise. The house was small and modest. They searched for cheap material, and with each swing of the hammer, they were one step closer to moving into their new home.

My grandfather was born on July 21, 1913. His name, Demos Shakarian.

The house was a plank house. Many of the floorboards did not even touch. That didn't matter to the newlyweds, as they moved in before it was even completed. It was my great-grandparents dream house because it was *their* home and they were thankful for it.

Though he had a family of his own, Great-Bobby Isaac supported his mother and all his sisters until the last sister was married. A short time later, he asked his mother to move into his home, where she would live out the rest of her days with her son and daughter-in-law. Because of his deep love for his mother and to honor his father, he happily continued providing for her.

MY GRANDFATHER IS BORN!

Soon Isaac and Zarouhi were blessed with a baby. Their first child, my grandfather, was born on Monday, July 21, 1913. Their son was named *Demos*, after Isaac's father and my great-great-grandfather. As Isaac looked at his tiny infant son, he knew he was blessed. The Lord had given him a son! *Demos is the seed of the one that came to America,* thought Isaac. *The Boy Prophet's words are coming true!*

With his son's birth came the beginning of a new era of blessing which would be revealed in the coming years. A time which would indeed fulfill the prophecy about "being a blessing to the nations."

"Without the influence of Demos Shakarian, countless men and women would not be involved in ministry today— or would not have the measure of effectiveness they have enjoyed in reaching the world with the gospel of Jesus Christ. I know this to be true, I am one of them.

As a young man growing up in a Christian home, I had an insatiable hunger for more of God. I remember searching the newspaper for advertisements of revival meetings and asking my parents if we could attend. Growing through the teen years in the tumultuous 70's, I sensed there had to be a way to receive more of God's power than I had known. I heard there was a church which had a reputation for miracles and supernatural demonstrations of God's presence. I went to see what I could find and got more than I expected. I experienced the mighty baptism in the Holy Ghost and the overwhelming power and presence of God which I had sought for years. My life was unalterably and irretrievably transformed. I didn't discover until later the church I visited, was strongly impacted by Demos Shakarian and his organization.

Demos was a humble man who had unshakable faith in a great God. He pursued the dream God gave him relentlessly. His obedience resulted in an ongoing harvest of productive lives and ministries, which will produce fruit until the coming of the Lord!

"The Shakarian Legacy" will encourage, challenge, and inspire you to do mighty exploits for the cause of Christ."

— Rod Parsley • Pastor / World Harvest Church, Host of *Breakthrough* / Chancellor, Valor Christian College

WORKING TOWARDS HIS DREAM

When my grandfather was eight months old, the family moved from the plank house in the heart of Los Angeles to their new home, a two-story white stucco Spanish-style house in the city of Downey. It was located on South Cerritos Ave, now known as Columbia Way. This was near where Great-grandfather used to buy the produce he sold and also the suburb where my grandfather would live his entire life.

The home was surrounded by eucalyptus trees, cornfields, and pastureland. Having extra space was wonderful for their ever-expanding family, as Isaac and Zarouhi were blessed with five daughters after their son Demos. Their names were: Ruth, Roxanne, Florence, Lucille, and Grace.

> "When I came to faith, the spiritual giants of that era included Demos Shakarian. His infectious and vibrant faith inspired my own and helped shape this young believer in Jesus. I'm grateful for his faithfulness to the Heavenly vision to reach the world with the Good News!"
> — **Chris Mitchell** • Middle East Bureau Chief / CBN News

Isaac continued to pursue his dream of establishing the largest independently owned Dairy Farm. With the economy flourishing, my Great-Bobby stepped out again and purchased 14 acres of land on Imperial Highway to expand his Dairy. Through his dairy farms, he significantly impacted Downey's commerce.

When he was still just a toddler, Grandfather learned how to milk a cow! In 1923, when Demos was ten years old the

10-acre-farm had been transformed into a 200-acre dairy farm. The original three cows my Great-Bobby Isaac began with, in 1913, had now grown to a herd of 500 cows. Great-

> *That cowboy hat turned into the famous cream-colored Stetson hat, his all-time favorite!*

Bobby was amazed each time he had a dream; it would come true! Since kneeling before the Bible years earlier, God delivered on every dream Isaac had. It was on this dairy farm that my grandfather first wore his much-loved *cowboy boots* and *hat*. Eventually, that cowboy hat turned into the famous *cream-colored Stetson hat*, his all-time favorite. Throughout his life, he was known for wearing this hat.

Isaac's next goal was to own and operate the largest and most successful dairy farm in the state of California. His family knew it would not be easy, but they were willing to work as hard as necessary to see his ultimate dream fulfilled, owning the largest dairy farm in the world!

> "Proverbs 29:18 tells us: 'Where there is no vision, the people perish ...'
>
> There is no man who knew that better than Demos Shakarian! Demos took the vision God gave him and impacted men, cities, and nations, one person at a time. His Christian values, business practices, integrity, and testimonies will forever leave an impression in the lives of the people he influenced. I have no doubt that his meetings were the genesis of the teachings of business and financial stewardship in the church today.
>
> Cynthia, congratulations on honoring your grandfather with, *The Shakarian Legacy*. He will always be remembered!"
>
> **— Carman Licciardello** • Recording Artist, Multiple GMA Dove Award Winner

CHAPTER FIVE

An Encounter
With The Holy Spirit

❧

*A*s a young boy, Grandfather knelt down in his father's fields and dedicated his life to the Lord. He told the Lord he would do whatever He asked him to do. It would be a defining moment in my Bobby's life!

The family attended the Armenian Pentecostal Church on Sunday mornings in Los Angeles. There Isaac's children were baptized and experienced divine healing and speaking in tongues. It created a strong foundation which would guide my family for many years to come. The Pentecostal experience would also make a huge mark on my grandfather's life as he became a successful businessman. Who would have known years later he would give birth to a worldwide Christian organization?

My family chose to travel to church by carriage. Even after all these years, their beloved horse Jack faithfully pulled the carriage, as he did when my Great-Bobby Isaac started selling produce. Everyone loved him, but no one more so than my Great-Bobby. Grandfather always spoke lovingly of Jack, who was treated with great care. When my Bobby was twelve, "Faithful Jack" was retired. He spent his final years enjoying some well-deserved luxury time in the pasture.

By 1926, my grandfather was thirteen years old. The Dairy herd had doubled again, numbering 1,000 dairy cows. With such increase and growth in the dairy business, it was necessary to hire additional help. Great-Bobby hired many Mexican-Americans to help his family with the growing duties of operating a dairy farm.

Isaac built a bunkhouse next to the barn for his employees. He also began to learn Spanish so he could communicate with them. As his fluency in Spanish increased, Isaac began telling stories to his employees about life in Armenia and how they came to this new land. My Great-Bobby was an excellent story-teller. Grandfather loved hearing these stories in Spanish, just as much as he loved hearing them in English. He committed them to memory and years later he would share them with me!

GRANDFATHER'S BROKEN NOSE

When Grandfather was ten years old and in the fifth grade, he broke his nose while working on his father's farm. Though I am sure he told me *how* it happened, I never did understand the exact details. I just remember thinking, *boys will be boys!* Sometime around thirteen years old, my grandfather found he was unable to hear as well as he once had. His mother took him to the doctor, who discovered my grandfather's nose had not healed correctly after the injury. Scar tissue was affecting his eardrums and significantly impaired his ability to hear.

Though he had two surgeries trying to correct his hearing problem, the operations were unsuccessful.

My Bobby was able to take a negative and turn it into a positive.

My grandfather's hearing loss meant he had to sit closer to the teacher to hear lectures in the classroom. It eventually limited his involvement in sports activities as well. Though, not even that would stop him. His broken nose turned into a blessing!

Throughout his life, my Bobby was able to take a negative and turn it into a positive. This was no exception. His hearing loss hindered his social life, as well as academically. He began taking extended time talking with the Lord. He would often lift his hands and pray asking God to allow him to hear more clearly. He especially loved worshipping and talking to the Lord privately, while walking through his father's cornfields.

> "To my view, the move of the Holy Spirit around the world from the 1950's and into the present, while ignited from heaven found hearts, which like torches began leading the 'spread of the flame.' Among these, no one exceeded the stewardship of that flame by faithfully leading sacrificially and creatively as Demos Shakarian.
>
> That God took a dairy farmer and energized a man's vision to penetrate the scope of the business world, the whole of the global church with the testimony of the truth of God's word, and the power of His Holy Spirit is remarkable. The credibility was sustained in this thrust through Demos' steadfastness to the testimony of Jesus, and the spirit of prophecy. By reason of consistency of character and avoidance of fanaticism, vibrant passion for God, and glorification of Jesus Christ was warmly alive, always with the companioning and confirming fire of God's Spirit and gifts among those gathered.
>
> It could well be said, that under God the Heavenly Father, Demos Shakarian was the foremost father among the many leaders around the world during those years."
>
> — **Jack Hayford** • Founding Pastor / Church on the Way,
> Chancellor / The King's University

MY SIMILAR JOURNEY

Like my grandfather who had a medical challenge, I too had a discovery at four-months-old. Doctors found I was born with a congenital heart condition. Cardiologists told my parents, I would likely need surgery before starting school. A team of physicians from White Memorial Hospital in Los Angeles gave examples of how my quality of life could be compromised. With the possibility of heart surgery, something no parent wants for their child; instead, my parents turned to God and prayed. My grandparents and Great-Bobby Isaac also kept it a matter of prayer and asked everyone they knew to pray for me as well. Wow, what a grand example of what was meant for evil, God turned around for good. How wonderful to have the avalanche of prayers continually being prayed over me at such a young age. I look back on it now with much gratefulness and gratitude!

As a child, I did not fully understand what the fuss was all about, especially because I, like my grandfather, also had limitations of activities at school put on me. What I do remember is feeling embarrassed as my mother continually pulled me into every healing line for prayer. As a result, I had amazing prayers, and anointings prayed over me. I was prayed for by Kathryn Kuhlman, Kenneth Hagin, and Oral Roberts, just to name a few.

> *I am thankful for my mother's diligence and my parent's faith in God.*

I am thankful for my mother's diligence and my parent's faith in God. They believed He would touch my life . . . and He did! I never had surgery, and no symptoms ever came. Instead, the anointed prayers of so many faithful people brought God's healing power.

Years later, continuing to have no symptoms, I was blessed with my beautiful daughter, Rachel Evangeline.

> "Church history shows us that a move of God happens when a man responds to Him. God is looking for those who will respond to Him so that the greatness of His plan can be fulfilled.
>
> Demos Shakarian is one of those men who through faith responded to God, and that response affected a generation. The fruit of his ministry is abundant and far-reaching.
>
> This book comes to you from the hands and heart of his granddaughter, Cynthia Shakarian, who saw it firsthand and recorded it for us to know.
>
> May the story of this precious man stir you to reach for more, and to run with the greatness of God's plan for your own life."
>
> **— Nancy Dufresne** • Dufresne Ministries

ANSWERED PRAYER

My Bobby was now thirteen in 1926, and longing to discover his purpose in life. Each Sunday was filled with charged anticipation, as something special almost always happened as believers came together. This day was no exception. As my Bobby entered the church, he began to feel different—as if a 'warm and comforting woolen blanket'—was slowly coming to rest upon his shoulders. He felt a heavy presence, and as he looked around, he was astonished to see that no one was near him. Moments later, he began to shiver. This feeling surprised him. He wasn't cold; he was warmed by an 'invisible heavy blanket' wrapped around him.

He said on this particular day; his heart was overflowing with a desire to talk with Jesus in a private, intimate way. As he opened his mouth to give a prayer filled with words of love for God, he heard words he did not understand. The words which came out were new and different. He was speaking a language he had never heard before. Somehow in his heart, he knew he was speaking words describing his deep love for Jesus. As this new language continued to flow, he realized he had been filled with the Holy Spirit.

He realized this power was something for all of God's children.

Being overwhelmed by the Lord's presence, people around were watching him and began to praise the Lord. The Spirit lingered with him for days after that miraculous morning at church. From that first day, a fire was lit which burned within Grandfather. Eventually, he would go on to introduce thousands of others to this Divine power.

At home in his bedroom, *God's presence* continued to linger on thirteen-year-old Demos. He described the encounter in such gentle terms. Although he didn't understand what was happening at the time, he was at peace. As my grandfather lay on the floor under this powerful Presence, he heard the Lord ask him three times, "This is my Power. Will you ever doubt it? What you are experiencing is Me." And each time he answered the Lord, "No, I will never doubt You!"

My grandfather knew he would never doubt the Lord again. The power which he felt around him was within him too, like electricity! He realized *this power* was something for all of God's children.

RECEIVING HIS HEALING!

At 5:00 in the morning his eyes opened. Instantly he noticed something was different! He had been awakened by the sound of birds chirping. Suddenly he real-ized he could hear! He received his miracle! Grandfather jumped out of bed, still in his clothes from the day before and hurriedly changed, before rushing out of his bedroom and down the long curved staircase. My grandfather did his chores around 5:30 in the morning, but this day he woke up much earlier. He couldn't wait to tell his parents about his miracle! As he found his way to the kitchen, he noticed he could hear his father turning the newspaper pages and his mother putting breakfast on the table. These sounds were music to his ears. He rushed into the kitchen shouting, "Mom! Dad! Guess what, I can hear!"

"You must have healed my hearing for an important reason."

My grandfather couldn't wait to be in his father's cornfields to spend time with God. He thanked the Lord for the incredible Divine miracle he had and for restoring his hearing. He whispered a prayer saying, "You must have healed my hearing for an important reason." He asked the Lord what that special reason was. What was his life's purpose?

"As a new believer, I was quickly introduced to the organization founded by Demos Shakarian. At the time it was one of the most powerful moves of God on the planet and gathered Christians from virtually every nation and denomination. Some of my most inspiring memories were attending Demos' events, and later speaking at them. I learned important truths, which became the foundation of my Christian walk. Truths taught by Demos, about loving God enough to share Him, and loving people enough to share our God with them. I have no doubt; he was one of the greatest men of God in his time. He had a major impact on not only his generation but everyone that will follow until the Lord returns!"

— **Rick Joyner** • Author of "The Final Quest" series

A MIRACLE

The doctor confirmed the change in my grandfather's hearing. Though it was not quite perfect, he was registering only ten percent hearing loss, which represented a miraculous improvement. Grandfathers' earlier hearing loss had affected his studies. He was two years behind his contemporaries in school. Although his academic achievement was not stellar; he was developing something else, an incredible sense for business.

In addition to his schooling, my grandfather worked hard helping his father with their thriving dairy farm. While Grandfather was attending high school; his father gave him 30 cows to manage so he could have the responsibility of running a dairy all on his own.

This was the beginning of what would become a successful business for my grandfather. In fact, while he was attending Downey High School, my grandfather asked one of his teachers to help him set up proper bookkeeping, including all the records necessary for a growing business. "My goodness! You are making more money than most of the teachers at the school!" His teacher pronounced when he saw what this sixteen-year-old boy was earning, with his small herd of dairy cows. The offspring was being blessed, just as the Lord promised so many years ago through the Boy Prophet.

Even as a teenager while attending high school and working long hours on the farm, my Bobby desired to please the Lord with every fiber of his being. As he continued to have success with his cattle, my grandfather dreamed of becoming a prophet

*He wanted to know,
What was
his purpose?*

or a preacher. Of course, he thought it would never come to pass. His heartfelt prayer was seeking God for direction in his life. He wanted to know, *What was he put on this earth to do?*

"Legacy is so important as the grace and blessing the Lord has given to us, are to be passed down not only to our natural families but to the family of God.

Demos Shakarian is a name which will be honored throughout history because he greatly exalted The Name Above All Names — Jesus Christ. As a new believer, I remember well the influence of this wonderful man of God. Throughout my years of maturing in Christ, his teaching, leadership, and encouragement, greatly strengthened and established my faith.

I am forever grateful. He left a legacy which is filled with the Lord's goodness and grace."

— Patricia King • Co-founder / XPmedia

CHAPTER SIX

Romance is in the Air

*A*s a teenager, my grandfather developed the skill of leading others while a Youth Leader at his church. It was during a service; he once again felt the "warm heavy blanket" experience. He knew that God's presence was on him. So he left the men's side of the congregation and walked over to his sister Florence, who had seriously broken her elbow. He laid his hand on his sister's arm and began praying for her healing. Later, when the Doctor removed the cast from her arm, he couldn't believe what showed on the x-ray. Her elbow looked like it had never been broken!

> "Demos' ministry gave me my first opportunity to speak.
> It was also my training ground as I heard other teachers.
> God really used Demos to impact the world for Jesus!"
> **— Sid Roth** • Host / *It's Supernatural!*

At thirteen years old, Grandfather experienced a Divine encounter with the Holy Spirit. Though it wasn't until something similar happened in my life, that I completely understood the power he had felt.

I was an adult the first time I felt this same gentle power flow into me. It was at an International Convention of my grandfather's organization. During this time, my father, Richard, was the International President. It happened after one of the evening meetings where Lance Wallnau was the guest speaker. His approach was different from other speakers I had heard. He integrated many "business principles" into his message. It was so insightful how he mixed business strategies with the Word of God. As I had never heard of him, I was pleasantly surprised to be so blessed by his message that night.

At thirteen years old, Grandfather experienced a Divine encounter with the Holy Spirit.

Though his message was inspiring, I didn't know that after the meeting I would be so personally touched. While in conversation with Lance, he asked if he could pray for my daughter and me. First, he prayed for my teenage daughter, Rachel, and then he prayed for me.

I don't remember entirely what he said, or what was so different from other prayers I had received. What I do remember in such vivid detail is what happened as he was praying. Suddenly, I felt a tremendous heat in my feet. The heat started moving slowly up my legs, and as it did, the heat greatly intensified. It continued to move up my body, slowly rising I felt the heat continuing to grow in strength until I felt as if a crown was placed upon my head. I remember feeling in complete shock and even greater joy at what I was experiencing.

This unexplainable phenomenon remained present for a few hours. It was as if *someone* had placed *something heavy* on top of my head. I could feel the weight of it, and the heat coming off of it. As if a tangible presence was resting there. Slowly, the intensity of the 'ring of heat on my head' lessened, as the minutes and hours passed.

My first *physical* encounter with the Holy Spirit was similar to my grandfather's; when he felt an 'invisible warm heavy mantle' wrapped around him. Grandfather often described his experience of being wrapped in a soft woolen blanket, tangibly heavy, but not uncomfortably so, and lingered for some time.

That is exactly how I would describe the presence which rested on my head. It was quite warm and heavy, but not uncomfortable. Though it was strange and new, I never wanted it to leave. This was not the first time I experienced the Holy

Wrapped in a soft woolen blanket, tangibly heavy, but not uncomfortably so.

Spirit, but it was the strongest tangible experience I have ever had with Him. At least as of the time I'm writing this. I would have given anything to have it last forever!

"I go way back with Demos from the early '70s. I loved Demos Shakarian and what he was doing. I loved the impact he had, not only on men but men, women, and families; and not only in America but all over the world. Those early days of my ministry are founded in his ministry. I still have fond memories today of the great impact of Demos Shakarian.

I'm excited that something new is happening with Demos' vision, and I'm glad that Cynthia Shakarian, the granddaughter of Demos, is listening to the Holy Spirit, and has decided it's time for his desire for unity, to become a vital part of what's happening in the world today. The vision of Demos Shakarian to spread God's love reached many people in the past, and I believe it will still reach many people in the days ahead."

— Jerry Savelle • Jerry Savelle Ministries International

DEMOS SPOTS HIS DREAM GIRL

My grandfather noticed a young lady in church. Though it was customary for the men to sit on one side, and the women to sit on the other, it didn't stop my grandfather from glancing over the aisle. He looked forward to Sundays because he just might catch a glimpse of Rose Gabrielian. Grandfather couldn't stop thinking about Rose. It was as though she appeared out of a dream. For the first time he thought, *I think I'm in love!*

During the week, when he thought about her his heart beat faster. When he was at Church, he looked for her, and when he would see her, he had to stop himself from staring. Little did he know that soon he would embark on a wonderful adventure . . . true love!

Rose's family lived in East Los Angeles, and whenever farm-related business took Grandfather anywhere nearby, he tried to find a reason to go past her family's home. It was an attempt to catch just a glimpse of Rose outside.

Armenian tradition did not permit interaction between a boy and girl unless they were married. So even if he had seen her, he could never have said anything to her. The custom was that a marriage was to be arranged by the parents. So for now he thought, *he will be satisfied with just catching a glimpse of her here and there.*

At nineteen years old when my grandfather was near graduation from high school, he decided to tell his parents about *the girl from church.* It occurred over a family dinner. Grandfather, all five of his sisters, and his parents were sitting around the dinner table. He was nervous, his hands fidgeting and suddenly his throat felt parched.

"Dad," he began by saying, clearing his throat once or twice before he continued. "I'm nineteen and a hard worker. And . . . ah . . . well . . . ah . . . Dad, I have a question for you. You were nineteen when you got married, right Dad?" The sisters immediately became silent and looked at their father, Isaac. His mother looked to her husband wondering, *what is this all about?* His father replied, "Yes, you're right. I was married at nineteen, but why are you asking?" Demos answered, "There is a girl I've seen, and I believe she's my wife."

Instantly, all his sisters jumped in singing, "Demos likes a girl! Demos likes a girl!" "And is this girl Armenian?" his mother continued. "Yes, she is," my grandfather nervously answered. "Is she a Christian, Demos?" his father said without skipping a beat. "Yes absolutely. She attends our church," Grandfather quickly proclaimed.

> *"Demos likes a girl! Demos likes a girl!"*

Again, he was met with silence. "It's Rose Gabrielian," my grandfather said, relieved to have spoken her name at last. While his younger sisters giggled, the older ones excitedly proclaimed, "Our big brother is in love!"

With that conversation, the traditional Armenian process of bringing two young people together in marriage began to unfold; between Grandfather's family and Rose Gabrielian's family. In later years the Gabrielians' would shorten their name, to Gabriel.

UNCLE JANOIAN

When arranging an Armenian engagement, the custom was the two families would not speak directly with one another.

A satisfactory go-between had to be selected to represent Great-grandfather Isaac. After a brief discussion between his parents, the family chose Raphael Janoian, the husband of Great-grandfather Isaac's sister, Siroon. He would speak to Mr. Gabrielian on behalf of Isaac.

Uncle Janoian owned a large junkyard, and the Gabrielian family had a refuse-hauling company. Because of their business connections, he and the Gabrielian family dealt with one another on a regular basis. This meant finding an appropriate time to speak to Rose's father wasn't a problem for him.

After the first meeting between Uncle Janoian and the Gabrielian family, my nineteen-year-old grandfather waited anxiously outside for his Uncle to return. When Uncle Janoian finally pulled into the driveway and parked the car, he walked straight past my grandfather not pausing to share the news of the meeting with him. He took his assignment very seriously

Isaac upon seeing his meticulously groomed son, did a double-take!

and was going to speak with Isaac first. After giving a friendly nod toward his nephew Demos, he entered the house and offered a greeting. He accepted some refreshments as he waited for Isaac and Zarouhi to join him.

Upon entering the room, they exchanged pleasantries then Uncle Janoian began speaking. Demos stood close-by listening, his heart pounding in anticipation. "Mr. and Mrs. Gabrielian has agreed to meet with your family next month. We have set a date for the meeting to occur." Demos was overjoyed at what he heard. They had said *yes* to the meeting! That must mean that Sirakan and Tiroon Gabrielian might perhaps agree to the marriage . . . or at least it may be a possibility!

The next month passed painfully slow for my grandfather. The meeting day could not come soon enough. When it finally arrived Grandfather finished all his chores as quickly as possible. He did not want to be late. Then he took several showers, careful to clean all the dirt from under his fingernails.

He wanted to be sure he was at his best, so he took his time and was meticulous. Putting on his best cowboy boots, soon it was time to leave. When Isaac saw his son, he did

Everyone found their seat in the family's canvas-topped black Packard.

a double-take because he had never seen him groomed so perfectly. My great-grandfather lovingly gave his son an approving smile. "Young love," Isaac murmured as everyone found their seat in the family's canvas-topped black Packard. It was much nicer than the carriage, but not loved nearly as much as old *Jack*, their beloved horse.

The journey felt to my grandfather as though it was the longest he had ever taken. Sitting in the crowded back seat along with his sisters, Demos could not wait to arrive at the Gabrielian residence. He was concerned his sisters rubbing against his shirt might wrinkle it.

THE PATRIARCHS SIT-DOWN MEETING

When the Shakarians' finally arrived, they got out of the car and made their way up the walkway toward the house. At the front door, they were greeted by Rose's parents, Sirakan and Tiroon Gabrielian. Standing beside them stood Rose's brother Edward, along with uncles, aunts, and many cousins. Grandfather looked right past all the faces. He was searching for Rose who stood behind her family in a beautiful rose-colored dress.

The Gabrielian's quickly welcomed the Shakarians' into their home and almost immediately, as dictated by custom, the men took their seats on one side of the room, and the women took their place on the other side.

As my grandfather gazed at all the people engaged in conversation in the big living room, he paused to observe his father Isaac and Mr. Gabrielian. They were seated away from the other men and deep in conversation. At some point, the two men stood up, which indicated it was time for the Shakarians' to leave. As Grandfather and his family moved toward the front door, he overheard Mr. Gabrielian say something to his father. "We will discuss it with Rose." Upon hearing those words, he was filled with excitement because he knew it was under consideration!

It was time for my Bobby to leave, but not before trying to sneak another glimpse in Rose's direction nonchalantly.

IT'S OFFICIAL! THEY'RE ENGAGED!

The weeks following seemed like months to my grandfather, as he anxiously awaited the news about Rose. When word finally came, he was overjoyed. Rose had agreed to marry him!

With this news, the traditional Armenian festivities began. This involved five nights of celebration at the home of the bride. Every evening featured something different. One night Rose gave a concert on the piano, and as Demos watched his future wife expertly playing, he felt blessed.

Everything was an expression of joy for the marriage which would take place between my grandparents. Through singing, words of congratulations, and eating, the families bound themselves together realizing the marriage was not solely between a young man and a young woman. It was between two families joining to build another bond as strong as their marriage.

Tradition established one of the evenings' events. The soon-to-be groom would give his fiancée a special gift selected by his parents as a symbol of love. The gift chosen for

Grandfather knew the importance of this moment!

my grandfather to give Rose on that very special night was a wristwatch surrounded by diamonds.

When it came time for my grandfather to give my grandmother this gift, young Demos stood and began the long journey across the living room. He took great effort not to trip on the Armenian rug that covered the floor. All the guests watched, as he walked from where the men were sitting in the room to the other side, where Rose sat with the women. Everyone knew this was a special moment for the couple and my Bobby felt the weight of his feet with each step. Not to mention, the weight of the importance of this moment!

When he finally reached Rose, he took the box out of his pocket which held the beautiful watch. My grandfather felt his heart pounding, as my grandmother raised her hand so he could place the watch around her wrist. He tried to secure the watch around Rose's delicate wrist, but he was "all thumbs." This was the closest he had ever been to Rose, and his heart was pounding. His big, rough farm hands could not manage to close the clasp. He fumbled, unsuccessfully, for what felt like an eternity. Without a word, Rose reached over gently with effortless grace to help her fiancé secure the clasp. It was the first time their hands touched!

THE SHAKARIANS & THE GABRIELIANS

As my grandfather's future began to unfold, his calling became more apparent. My grandmother would also have a significant role in his destiny. The five-day celebration at the Gabrielian's home was in full swing, and at last, it was time to marry.

Doesn't this generation understand Armenian traditions?

As relatives of the two families celebrated the future marriage of Demos and Rose, the details of the matrimonial union were also negotiated. It was determined Rose must wait until she was sixteen years of age to wed. This was, to my grandfather's dismay, more than a year away.

The families also agreed to hold the wedding at my grandfather's family home. In real Armenian fashion, a huge sit-down dinner for all the guests would immediately follow. It was decided the reception would be on Isaac's double tennis courts. Even the details of the meal would be mutually agreed upon. The menu would include *shish kabob, wedding pilaf* with dates, almonds, and raisins. There would be plenty of *hummus, string cheese, lavash* (flatbread), *baba ganoush* (eggplant), *lahmajoon*, along with many pastries, including *baklava* and *shakar lokum*. Of course, my great-grandmother also made her now-famous *dolmas*.

ALONE AT LAST ... AND SPEECHLESS

Grandfather anxiously awaited permission to speak to Rose for the first time, but as the five nights of celebration were coming to an end, he still had not spoken to his soon-to-be bride.

With total disregard for Armenian custom, my grandfather suddenly looked over in Mrs. Gabrielian's direction and blurted out a request for permission to speak with Rose. Mrs. Gabrielian seemed shocked by his request. Then she shook her head, not as a denial, but as if to say: *Doesn't this generation understand Armenian traditions?*

"Rose, I know God wants us to be together!"

Nonetheless, Mrs. Gabrielian led Demos and Rose into the next room. Placing two chairs in the center of the room, she made sure they were still far apart. She motioned for her daughter and soon-to-be son-in-law to take their seats. And with that, Mrs. Gabrielian left the room. But she kept the door wide open!

Before taking his seat, young Demos held the chair for Rose to be seated. Once he sat down, he tried to remember all the magnificent words he had planned to say to her.

I have prayed those would be the first words the man I marry would speak to me.

He had practiced these lovely words so many times in his mind, and in front of the bathroom mirror. Now, the moment was finally here. This was the moment he had been dreaming of for so long. He could finally express to Rose how he felt, saying ... Oh No! ... Wait!

A DIVINE INTERVENTION

What was he going to say? He sat there, speechless! With Rose sitting next to him in her chair, the silence seemed to last forever. His mind kept racing as he tried to retrieve *just one* of the beautifully articulated phrases he was planning so carefully to say, but nothing happened! When he finally opened his mouth to speak, he had completely forgotten everything he had rehearsed. All the lovely words he had planned to express his love, gave way to this statement, "Rose, I know God wants us to be together!" As my grandfather heard the words come out of his mouth, he paused and looked at Rose, still in disbelief at what he had said to her.

Much to his amazement, a huge smile came across Rose's face, and my grandfather saw love shining in her eyes. "All of my life, I have prayed those would be the first words the man I marry would speak to me," she said softly.

My grandfather's befuddled words were nothing short of an answer to my grandmother's prayers. Even in such a significant time of intense emotion, Grandfather was led by the Holy Spirit. And with those words, the Lord confirmed their relationship and their destiny was sealed. Alone in the room, seated on the two chairs purposely separated, they began a life together. They both loved God and wanted to serve Him. Yet they never imagined at that moment, the magnitude of what God had in mind for them to accomplish!

"Demos Shakarian and his precious wife, Rose, touched my life deeply. Back in the '70s when I would speak at his Conventions, my life was enriched. I would not be where I am and who I am, had it not been for Demos and Rose Shakarian.

Demos' meetings have left a mighty mark on the church worldwide. I will never forget being with Demos in Toronto, seeing the love of God in his life was overwhelming and life-changing. I saw firsthand the impact Demos had in Canada where I lived, and in cities like New York, Miami, and other places where I would go . . . it was mighty!

I saw God's power manifest in such an awesome way. I still remember the anointing of the Holy Spirit and the miracles I witnessed with my own eyes. I treasure my memories of those times.

Demos Shakarian touched my life in a profound way! His legacy continues today through his son, Richard, and granddaughter Cynthia Shakarian. Only eternity will reveal the countless lives he touched for God's glory."

— **Benny Hinn** • Pastor / Benny Hinn Ministries

CHAPTER SEVEN

A Wedding to Remember

*I*n the Armenian culture, engagement parties are larger than most people's weddings. Rose and Demos' engagement celebration was no exception. The sit-down dinner hosted about 300 guests, and it included all of the trimmings. It was held in a grocery store, which was owned by the Gabrielians and beautifully decorated for the occasion. This celebration was held shortly after Demos and Rose had their first conversation.

Leading up to the ceremony the traditions were in full force, and this was every bride's dream. The responsibility of the groom's family was to purchase the bride's complete wardrobe for the wedding. Not only for during the engagement and the wedding, but for the entire first year of marriage: including dresses, shoes, hats, and gloves. After all these preparations, my grandfather would then finally place the engagement ring on Grandmother's finger.

THE "EARHART" CONNECTION

It's important to note how much tradition played a role in this process. When it was time to select the diamond ring for Rose, my grandfather did not purchase a diamond engagement ring on his

The mother of the famous pilot Amelia Earhart.

own. Grandfather and Grandmother, accompanied by Great-grandmother and a number of relatives, all went to look for the ring which was to be given to Rose by Demos. Tradition!

The family traveled to downtown Los Angeles in search of the perfect engagement ring. In one of the stores, they were helped by Mrs. Amy Earhart, the mother of the famous pilot, Amelia Earhart. She would become the first female aviator to fly solo across the Atlantic Ocean.

Mrs. Earhart was very proud of her daughter, and the family listened to her talk about Amelia, as my great-grandmother Zarouhi selected the diamond ring. In keeping with tradition, the decision was not open for discussion and was made solely by the mother of the groom. As Grandfather heard the woman talk about her daughter, he had no idea how often he would hear the name Amelia Earhart in future years!

THEIR DREAM WEDDING!

After the ring had been purchased, the engagement party came together quickly. Over three-hundred guests sat down to a full Armenian feast to celebrate the engagement of Demos and Rose. My grandparents couldn't wait for the wedding. It was a full year away. Grandfather spent this time working hard tending to his cattle and saving money to start his life with my grandmother.

The wedding between my grandparents took place on August 6, 1933. He was 20, and she was 16. As was the custom, the groom's family picked up the bride from her home and brought her, to *his home* for the wedding.

Early in the morning, a parade of cars decorated with flowers and streamers, drove to the Gabrielian home to pick up my grandmother. The Gabrielian family joined the procession making an even larger parade of 25 festive cars. They returned to the Shakarian home in Downey, where the wedding ceremony took place. The Shakarian property had been transformed by relatives into a magical wonderland; with sparkling lights, candles, and flowers everywhere, including roses. It was a grand celebration with over 500 guests attending.

As Grandfather watched my petite grandmother slowly walk down the aisle towards him, he became overwhelmed with thankfulness to the Lord for blessing him with such a beautiful bride. As the sun set all the candles twinkled, transforming it into a beautiful fairy-tale wedding.

There was an extraordinary silence, as their vows echoed. In reverence, they knelt on their knees to receive communion. The candlelight was casting a glow upon them. It made them appear angelic as if God's glory was draped over them. Great-grandfather Isaac stepped up in front of my grandparents, placing his hand on their heads, he prayed a blessing over their marriage.

It made them appear angelic as if God's glory was draped over them.

The blessing included Deuteronomy 28:1-14. The same Bible verses the Lord had given Isaac at fourteen-years-old. Also, the same Bible verses prayed over my great-grandparents, Isaac and Zarouhi at *their wedding.*

The wedding proved to be the social event of the year. It was reported in many popular newspapers of that day. The 500 wedding guests, including business people and top officials, enjoyed delicious Armenian food. Great-grandmother Zarouhi prepared many of the dishes. The celebration lasted well into the night as the guests danced the traditional Armenian circle dance. Guests read poems which had been specially written for the couple. Traditional speeches were given, and everyone wished Demos and Rose a beautiful long and happy marriage.

At the end of the evening, my grandparents looked at one another their eyes expressing the joy their hearts felt, knowing they were finally married and would spend the rest of their lives together.

They left for their honeymoon, now united in marriage with a shared sense of purpose. Not realizing, that soon they would embark on their greatest adventure ever. They were excited about their future and wondered where God would take them. Little did they know . . . He had big plans for them!

> "I remember sitting in the home of Demos and Rose. We had so many questions about the great moves of God which they had been a part of. Rose would play the piano, and we would ask Demos questions. It impacted our lives as young ministers forever.
>
> Demos and Rose had the ability to see potential in a person's call! He had a way of never separating between one person who loved Jesus and another. This made a lasting impartation into our lives. We can never thank God enough for their generosity.
>
> Our father in the faith, Dr. Lester Sumrall, taught us about the 'germination of pure faith from one generation to the next.' This is the legacy of Demos and Rose Shakarian as their work continues even now. Their heart's desire is to see people of all nations and all lovers of Christ be united in one strong, mighty body, The Church!"
>
> **— Robin Harfouche** • Christian Harfouche, Global Revival

EXPANDING THE BUSINESS

Traditions are strong and extend beyond the engagement and wedding ceremony, to also dictate the protocol *after the wedding*. At the time my grandparents were married the custom was that a newly married couple were to live with the groom's

Their first child,
my father Richard,
was born.

parents for at least the first year. This was true for my grandparents.

Their first child, my father Richard, was born October 23, 1934, while Demos and Rose were living with Isaac and Zarouhi.

About this same time, Demos and Rose started building a home next door to Isaac's large white Spanish-style stucco home. Because my grandfather and his father worked together in the dairy business, building a home close together was convenient, this was their way of life and also based on tradition. The properties were originally on Lexington – Gallatin Road, in Downey. Eventually, the two homes were relocated at 8417 Lexington Road and 8413 Lexington Road, where they still stand today.

Isaac reached his goal of becoming the *largest independently owned dairy farm in California*. His goal was met, but Isaac was working toward his ultimate dream. He needed to expand the herd to at least 3,000 milking cows to accomplish his ultimate goal, which had not yet ever been achieved!

AN ENTREPRENEUR

Holding this dream deep within his heart, this hard-working Armenian dairy farmer was determined to build *the largest independently owned dairy farm in the world*!

Building the dairy was his number one business priority, but the dairy also branched into other entities like hauling milk, raising hogs, and packing meat. What warmed Great-grandfather's heart was not just the expansion of his dream. It was also because of the many families he was able to help in the 1930's, by providing them employment. Isaac also encouraged and assisted his brother-in-laws to start their own businesses.

During the height of the Depression, my family faced obstacles which included labor disputes. They began to branch out by establishing the Great Western Milk Transport Company, which featured 400 milk tankers. They also started a meat packing plant in Downey, called the Great Western Packing Company. It was run by Great-Bobby Isaac's brother-in-law, Tom Kardashian. Tom was the husband of Isaac's little sister, Hamas, and the grandfather of Attorney Robert Kardashian.

As a successful businessman, my Great-Bobby Isaac became involved in the community, eventually becoming President of the Downey Chamber of Commerce. With his string of successful companies, many in the community came

> *Wealthy or poor received the same elaborate meal on the same beautiful china!*

to Great-Bobby, Isaac's home every week. Isaac and Zarouhi hosted dinner parties for many prominent people, including politicians and business leaders. Their guests feasted on delicious Armenian dishes, all prepared by Great-grandmother.

I can only imagine when she was a young bride marrying a man who had just begun to make a livable salary, she had no idea she would soon be entertaining the "Who's Who in California." But oh, how they all loved her cooking, especially her *dolmas*!

My great-grandparents were extremely caring to others and often invited people to dinner who had suffered a hardship or loss. Great-Bobby was a man of great compassion and remembered how he had struggled in the weeks and months following his father's death. He recalled his chronic cough and the horrible conditions in the harness shop. So my great-grandparents made sure all of their guests, wealthy or poor, received the same elaborate meal prepared and served on the same beautiful china!

Isaac and Zarouhi, as well as Demos and Rose, realized their success came from God. Just like "the blessing" prophesied by the Boy Prophet back in Kara Kala. My great-grandfather and grandfather always acknowledged the Lord in everything they did. They never forgot how far God had taken them. They also embraced the American dream. Believing that hard work joined with their faith in God (their key ingredient), could make their dreams into a reality!

"Demos Shakarian represented the scriptural truth that wealth is gained by following the principles of economics which include education, creativity, hard work, and opportunity. This is of God."

— **Noel Jones** • Bishop / City of Refuge, Featured on *Preachers of L.A.*

RELIANCE DAIRY

With his complete reliance on God to direct him in every decision, Isaac named his farm "Reliance Dairy." Helping with the growth of the family dairy business, Grandfather took on the responsibility of a new dairy operation, called "Reliance Number Three." Eventually, this company took on milking facilities, a creamery, and ice cream plant. Later they would expand even larger by opening drive-in stores.

Isaac named his farm "Reliance Dairy."

My Bobby went on to own two 800-acre ranches in Northern California, and he became a major Southern California real estate developer. It seemed as though most of the property he bought miraculously turned into "prime land" once my grandfather purchased it. As others watched this occurrence, they were amazed time and time again. He carried the attitude he learned from his father, Isaac. He depended entirely on God. He chose to pray about every decision connected with running the dairy business; from what property he bought to purchasing livestock.

Grandfather never did spend hours and days picking out a bull as most cattlemen did. Instead, he would walk-in and wait for God to *shine a light* on one of the bulls. Once Demos saw the bright shining light on a bull, he purchased it. "That's the one!" he would tell the salesperson. "Are you sure?" the salesman would ask. "Yes! That's the one." Sometimes Grandfather would not even look at all the bulls available for purchase before making his decision.

The salesmen were never comfortable with Grandfather's quick decision-making process, and they would often ask more questions. "Oh, come on Demos! How do you know which one to choose? Most dairymen look over all the bulls for days and seek expert opinions on which one to buy. Do you have an inside agent?" they jokingly asked Grandfather. "I sure do!" he would say. He explained that he prayed first to God for direction than prayed over his cows, the price of alfalfa, his fleet of trucks for hauling milk and all decisions relating to his business. He raised quite a few eyebrows from his reply!

Other dairymen did not understand my grandfather's business practices either. He seemed to make quick and impulsive decisions about livestock, often choosing what appeared to be the smallest bull. However, as Grandfather said on more than one occasion, he never based his decision on the size of the animal or the ancestry. Often a blue-ribbon pedigree bull would sell for top dollar going for over $50,000, with no guarantee that the offspring would be of equal or greater pedigree.

Instead, Grandfather chose to partner with God, praying and asking Him to reveal which bull would be the "champion breeder." Grandfather trusted that God was directing his decision in the purchase of a bull for breeding purposes, to expand his herd. Not surprisingly, Grandfather's choice

Pabst Leader was Grandfather's favorite and most productive bull!

transmitted into building a high-quality herd of cows over and over again. Demos helped Isaac grow the family business, purchase additional trucks and come one step closer to fulfilling their dream of expanding Reliance Dairy, to be the *largest independently owned dairy in the world*!

PABST LEADER

One of the bulls which would help them with this dream was named "Pabst Leader." He was purchased by Grandfather because the light shined brighter on Pabst than it had on any other bull. Grandfather paid $5,000 for him, but he became worth so much more. Pabst Leader was forever Grandfather's favorite and most productive bull!

Does it sound strange my grandfather knew his bull was a blessing from God? Well, you'll understand after reading this story, which was recounted by a precious friend. Her parents were great friends with my grandparents.

When Rebecca was a young girl, she went with her family to visit my grandfather on one of our farms. She was amazed how huge the dairy farm was. Rebecca saw cows as far as her eyes could see. She was also surprised by the strange request which Grandfather made of her family.

> *Grandfather loved and prayed for his cows!*

My grandfather loved his cows and continually prayed over them. He prayed they would be disease-free. He prayed they would be the biggest milk-producing cows and the healthiest cows that anyone had ever seen! Since he knew Rebecca's family was a powerful prayer family, he asked them on that sunny California day to pray for his cows too. *Okay,* young Rebecca thought. *We will stand here and pray for his cows.*

Well, that was not exactly what my grandfather had in mind. To Rebecca's surprise, my grandfather began taking the family to each cow so her anointed father along with their family could pray for them. He wanted to make sure every single one of his cows was blessed, so he walked the entire property until every last cow received their anointing.

Rebecca shared with me what an impression my grandfather's passion for prayer made on her as a young girl. I understood exactly what she meant. Reflecting back I realize, observing Grandfather has impacted me in ways for which I will always be thankful.

HOLY COW! THEY ARE HEALED!

Aimee Semple McPherson was a Christian Evangelist who experienced great miracles of healings in her services and founded the *Foursquare Church*. When she passed away, Kelso Glover filled her position. Grandfather would have lunch with him and talk about his passion for fulfilling his purpose on this earth. But what was amazing is how their friendship began.

A disease was found in my Bobby's dairy cows! Many dairymen in Southern California lost their entire herd due to the Tuberculosis Plague, which was running rampant through the cows. Several herds in surrounding areas had already been destroyed. When a percentage of cows in a single herd was found to be infected with the plague, the state of California would step in and demand the entire herd be put down.

This particular herd of Grandfather's totaled 1,000 cows. The state had already come in and tested the herd. Many of the cows showed they were infected. If there was even one more cow showing signs of the disease when the state came back to test again, the whole herd would be put down. This would be financially devastating. Though Grandfather was concerned with the financial consideration, he also loved his cows and did not want to see them harmed in any way.

My Bobby and his Dad, my Great-Bobby stayed up into the night discussing the situation. They knew how easily the disease spread once its germ was found in even a few. In fact, every other herd they had ever known which had so many cows testing positive for the disease, had been destroyed. They needed God to move in this situation. They needed God to save their cows!

> *To honor God they kept their hats off.*

They were both feeling pretty low by this point and felt they had exhausted their prayers, and were physically worn out. Needing some encouragement, they turned on the radio to listen to an inspiring message. What they heard was a sermon on "God's healing power over every disease," by Dr. Kelso Glover.

The next morning my grandfather called Dr. Glover and asked if he believed God's power could heal animals too. He confirmed, *he believed it was for everything on this earth.* My grandfather asked him if he could come over to the dairy farm and pray for his cows. Grandfather asked Kelso Glover to lay hands on his cows. With the power of agreement, Kelso Glover and my grandfather prayed, "Lord, the cattle on a thousand hills are Yours. In the name of Jesus, we take authority over Tuberculosis and every disease in the cows. I pray that all the cows are completely free of all diseases." Then Dr. Glover *came against every germ that would even try to touch these cows.*

I was impressed once again with my grandfather's integrity and desire to honor God, as he continued the story. He explained, even though it was a sweltering day and they spent hours in the sun going around the entire property praying for all the cows, both men kept their hats off, which would typically be protecting them from the heat. They wanted to be respectful because they were talking to their Heavenly Father. Their desire to give honor to God was stronger than trying to protect their heads from the sun.

Now instead of dreading for the state to come back to the dairy farm, he welcomed them. He was excited because he knew in his heart his cows were completely disease free.

Upon returning the inspectors said, "How did this happen? You had many in your herd infected with the disease, and now not even one of them is infected. I am giving all your cows a clean bill of health."

Even decades later my families cows were disease free!

"Honoring Our Past Opens Up Our Future!

The legacy of Demos Shakarian continues in the hearts of many today. I am one of those.

Being prophetic causes you to seek out where the Spirit of God is moving. The Lord baptized me in the Spirit in 1972. Even though I was young and did not fully understand what had happened, the prophetic gift in me began to come alive. Thankfully, there was someplace your gift felt welcomed; in Demos' meetings. I can honestly say without it; I am not sure I would have fully recognized and nurtured the gift that was within me.

The legacy continues in my heart, as I travel throughout the world releasing the Word of God to key leaders and the body of Christ in many nations. I thank God for Demos Shakarian, who has gone before us to pave the way for the Spirit to continue to manifest."

— **Chuck D. Pierce** • President, Global Spheres Inc. / Glory of Zion International

CHAPTER EIGHT

Created With a Special Purpose!

❦

*A*t 15, I, like all my girlfriends were influenced by the singer Cher. I made sure my long brown hair was as straight as it could be, and I would comb it just like hers. My friends would giggle every time I would swoosh my hair as Cher does. They would tell me I looked like her and I felt so cool!

At that time, though I thought I was so "grown up," my grandmother and I continued our tradition of going to *McDonald's*. I never felt too cool for *that* and enjoyed every moment with her. She had the best laugh. Everything seemed to amuse her and I'm sure I, her Cher-looking groovy granddaughter, was one of them!

We would head to the Downey McDonald's at the intersection of Lakewood Boulevard and Florence Avenue for lunch, which we considered a treat, or at least I did. I later learned this was one of McDonald's very first locations.

My mother seldom took me to fast food restaurants because she preferred healthier options, a wise choice in retrospect. Nonetheless, visiting McDonald's with my grandmother was always fun. A Cheeseburger, French Fries, and a Chocolate Shake was my standard order. We would take our food home and eat at my grandparents' dining room table ... enjoying every bite!

I loved hearing Grandmother Rose's version of the stories regarding our family history. As I unwrapped my cheeseburger from its yellow-coated-paper wrapping, Grandmother would tell me her side of the stories. They always had that awesome Momie twist on them. It was *a girl thing*!

FAITHFUL MILTON

My Bobby's entire life seemed to be a string of incredible events. This made hearing about a supernatural experience which involved a precious man in his life named Milton, so remarkable. It taught me how God may have someone prophesy about your life and follow it up with a confirmation later. This is what happened to Grandfather.

Bobby loved working with his Dad and building toward their dream of becoming, the largest independently owned dairy farm in the world. At the same time, something within him longed to give back to God for all the blessings in his life. My Bobby said he often felt as if he were on the receiving end of the blessings rather than the giving end. This became an inner struggle. He was also puzzled by a prophecy given to him by a man named Milton Hanson. Milton was a Norwegian house painter whom God used in an amazing way in my Bobby's life.

One evening Milton was over at my grandparent's home. He was a cheerful man, humming gospel songs as he painted. As they visited with him, the Norwegian house painter began to speak in an authoritative voice, telling my grandparents "they were chosen vessels." Milton continued, "You are being guided by the Lord," he said, speaking louder as he went on. "Keep

What God is opening up to you, no man can stop!

your mind on the things of God, and God will continue to guide you. God is going to use you mightily. Soon many cities and countries will open up to you, and you will share things of God with heads of state. What God is opening up to you, no man can stop!"

My grandparents looked at each other in disbelief. They were stunned by the words Milton spoke. Grandfather wondered, *What would bring a dairy farmer together with heads of state?*

As my grandparents sat there speechless, Milton rushed to an explanation. "I'm only telling you what God has shown me! I don't understand what I'm saying any more than you do. I'm just telling you what I heard."

A DIVINE CONFIRMATION

Strangely, what Milton said wasn't the only unusual encounter Grandfather had that week. Reflecting on it now, I can see how God was gently leading Grandfather in the direction He wanted him to go.

Grandfather explained the story like this:

"Milton's words were so confusing to me until God confirmed his words a few days after his visit. At the last minute and on what I thought was an impulse; I decided to attend a Wednesday night service at a church I had never attended previously. As the altar call was given, I suddenly found myself at the front of the church kneeling with tears streaming down my checks. Although I was a Christian, I wanted more of

God and less of me. I was spending all my time from sunrise to sunset on building the dairy business. Even most of my prayers had to do with the dairy.

I knew in my heart though I loved Him, God was not my priority. I had a desire deep within to do more for God but didn't know what He wanted me to do. So I went forward and knelt at the altar praying God would show me.

As I prayed at the altar, I suddenly sensed the pastor approaching. He came over to me and laid his hands on my head. His voice suddenly took on a quality which was reminiscent of Milton's authoritative voice, as he said:

'God has chosen you for a very special job to do. HE will be with you and direct you each step of the way. You will be with heads of state and government officials and share the Lord with them. The doors God is opening up to you, no man can shut."

Grandfather was stunned by the words the pastor had spoken. How could it be that the pastor of the church and Milton the house painter had said words so similar? Yet, the words he had declared with such authority, were almost verbatim to the words Milton had spoken to him a few days earlier.

> "You will be with heads of state and government officials and share the Lord with them."

Up to this time, my grandfather's focus had been on running Reliance Dairy. As he knelt in prayer that night, he wondered, *Could God be giving me a Divine directive? Letting me know what He wants me to do?* It was definitely much more than a coincidence.

"Demos Shakarian was one of those rare individuals who anticipated the future prior to its arrival. By faith, he brought that future into present reality by cooperating with the Holy Spirit. There would be little or no emphasis at all today on 'market-place ministry' without Demos' determination to build a coalition a generation ago: of business owners and entrepreneurs who loved God and wanted to make a difference in the corporate cultures, and entrepreneurial settings in society.

His ministry held to a Kingdom vision for what God can do in the business world when Kingdom values of faith, hope, and love are foundational to the marketplace, and where Jesus' Lordship is unapologetically honored. Demos expanded the awareness of the Church and invited us all to take what we have been given outside the four walls of our Sunday gatherings, into the day to day affairs of commerce and trade.

For believers, the business landscape has forever been shifted because of Demos Shakarian's pioneering faith and cutting-edge future thinking!"

— **Mark Chironna** • Pastor / Church on the Living Edge

SEARCHING FOR HIS PARTICULAR GIFT AND HEARING MINE!

In the following months, my grandparents were blessed with the birth of a beautiful little girl, Geraldine Shakarian. "Geri" as they called her, was born October 24, 1938. She was a much-welcomed addition to their family. My grandparents were thrilled to have their baby girl! Sometime after Geri's birth came a large family gathering, which had a profound impact on Grandfather.

At the gathering, as Demos looked around the room he realized that most of the guests were the offspring of those who had fled Armenia. This fact struck him. They all were tremendously blessed and prospered in this new land, as the "Boy Prophet" back in Armenia had foretold. He reflected on the details of the prophecy which said: "Those who left Armenia and went to the West Coast would be blessed along with their seed, and God would cause them to be a blessing to the nations."

He had indeed prospered, but was he blessing others enough?

As he reflected upon these words; he had indeed prospered, but was he blessing others enough? Was he really doing everything he could to help other people? Was his blessing sufficient to bless nations? Since the prophecy about leaving Armenia had come to pass, he wondered; *when the recent prophecies he received would come to fruition.*

As he started focusing on the world around him, my Bobby began to see that God was directing his life. He noticed other people's relationship with God was different. It appeared they didn't know God intimately as he did. He realized he was surrounded by individuals who needed to hear about the love of the Lord. He looked past the rough exterior of the cowhands and truck drivers and saw their heart. Maybe, he thought, *this is the special job God has for me.*

Years later my Bobby would tell me; I believe God has a particular gift for each one of us – a unique ability we are to use for His Kingdom. Then he paused and looked at me with those big loving eyes and said:

"That means you too, Cynthia! I see great things in you. God has blessed you with the ability to relate to people from all walks of life. Your compassionate heart and soft-spoken manner draw people in. The gifts God has given you will impact nations!"

A VISION OF DESTINY

While still contemplating and talking with God about exactly how he could go about reaching out to others, a picture of Lincoln Park suddenly came to him. Lincoln Park was filled with trees and open green spaces. Families would take bread to the duck ponds on weekends and toddlers ran squealing with glee down the hills. Young adults would meet up with their friends for picnics. It was a big park where people loved to gather, especially on beautiful summer weekends.

Unfortunately, what Grandfather saw during his evening prayer was utterly terrifying to him. He saw himself in the middle of a crowd of people who were seated on the ground. He stood there, wearing his Stetson hat, of course. What was so frightening to him, was all those people were there to hear him speak!

He wasn't a public speaker, and he knew it. Though he had incredible business sense, he spoke slowly because he was thoughtful in what he was saying. Rarely did he want to talk to more than a few people at a time. He considered himself an ordinary dairy farmer. This reminded me of Moses when God called him at a time when Moses was not confident of his speaking abilities.

Realizing this was *definitely not* the answer he had been waiting for, Grandfather dismissed the images he saw in his mind, while trusting God would show him what He wanted him to do. Unfortunately for my grandfather, days later the images were still just as vivid in his mind. Troubled by the lingering images, he decided to mention it to Grandmother.

As he started to explain in detail about how he had visualized himself speaking to a large crowd of people sharing the love of God, he added, "You'll never guess where all this was taking place?" To my grandfather's surprise, my grandmother responded with confidence, "Lincoln Park?" She went on to reveal that God had been talking to her about the same thing. This was *not* what my grandfather wanted to hear! He began listing the reasons this could not be a real possibility. He reminded my grandmother he was not a public speaker. "I am a dairy farmer!" he said. "I am a businessman!" he proclaimed. "What do I know about public speaking?"

My grandmother overlooked Grandfather's concerns and reminded him how they had been asking God to show them what they were to do for Him. "If this is truly God's idea it will work out," she assured him. "You have nothing to worry about. How could we both have the same idea at the same time if God did not direct this? There is no way this can be a coincidence. It must be from God!"

"When I first committed my life to Christ in 1972 a close friend of mine took me to one of Demos' meetings to hear great men of God speak. I was immediately hooked. From that time on, I went to countless numbers of meetings organized and directed by this great man of God.

I can say beyond a shadow of a doubt, this man and his great organization were a part of laying a strong foundation for me in the early years of my faith walk. I am doing my best to live by the principles of character, and integrity this great man of God stood for and taught to people all over the world.

I am so thankful Cynthia Sharkarian was chosen to write this book about her grandfather's life and remind all of us of his legacy which lives on!"

— Nancy Alcorn • President / Mercy Ministries

BEHIND EVERY GREAT MAN

As she shared with me Grandfather's concern about public speaking, I felt nervous for him just thinking about it because I had to admit, I felt the same way. My insides were churning just imagining his anguish!

Momie did not let up about holding a meeting at Lincoln Park. Bobby finally went to check with the city. He wiped the sweat from his brow in relief, upon learning that Lincoln Park was not available for a meeting. It was for public use only.

Momie did not let this stop her. She did some investigating on her own and discovered an empty lot near the park. It was available for rent on Sunday afternoons.

Grandfather was so happy Lincoln Park was unavailable, and he was even more relieved he didn't have to be the center of attention.

I can only imagine the look on Grandfather's face when my grandmother told him about the vacant lot, which *was available!*

Fortunately, everything after that moved so fast Grandfather had little time for concern. The images which God had put in his mind were now becoming a reality, and there was so much for him to do to prepare for the day. Permits were needed, a platform set up with microphones and so much more.

A date was set for the summer in the early 1940s. As the date approached . . . fear tugged at him. *What might go wrong? Will my reputation be ruined if I make a fool of myself? Will a work colleague be in the crowd? What if people misunderstand my message? Will I cause damage to the Dairies my father has worked so hard to build?*

SUNDAY AFTERNOON AT THE PARK

Grandmother was found smiling from ear to ear on the day
her husband was going to speak. She was giddy with excitement,
dressed in her Sunday best. Grandfather on the other hand . . .
was praying for rain!

All of a sudden the memories came flooding back to the
first day when he was alone with his
bride-to-be. He remembered being
tongue-tied and feeling so awkward.
He thought about how he had prepared that beautiful and sentimental
speech for Rose, which he had rehearsed over and over. Yet,
everything he planned to tell her went right out the window.
What came out instead were the same words she had prayed to
hear from the man who would be her husband.

Grandfather on the other hand, was praying for rain!

Now, years later, on the platform at the vacant lot on a beautiful sunny Southern California day, the same thing happened.
My grandmother began playing the piano leading the crowd in
gospel hymns. Then my Bobby stood on the platform and spoke
from his heart. He trusted the Lord would speak through him
and direct the meeting. As he continued talking, he noticed
something which upset him. A couple who had been sitting on a
colorful picnic blanket stood up. Then another young couple did
the same thing. He panicked, *why were they leaving?*

After a few minutes, he realized the exact opposite was
happening. The onlookers were getting closer so they could hear
what he had to say. Once he realized people were moving toward
him and not away from him, he began to gain momentum. He
believed no one knew his name, or so he thought. He decided

to pick one smiling face in the crowd and to focus on that face. As he was talking to this one person, he heard someone call his name. His eyes darted from person to person. Who was here who knew his name? To his dismay, he saw the face of a man with whom he conducted business. *Oh dear,* he thought. *This isn't going to end well. Where's the exit?*

CLOSER TO HIS PURPOSE

Just as Grandfather was ready to run, his attention was diverted. In front of him stood the same smiling man upon whom Grandfather had first focused his eyes. The man had tears running down his face and was so touched by my grandfather's message.

My grandmother Rose quietly invited the man onto the platform. Now standing next to my grandfather, the man took the microphone, much to Grandfather's complete relief, and started sharing his successes and also his failures. He said after listening to what my grandfather had to say, he realized it was a personal relationship with the Lord he was missing in his life. More people started to gather around to hear what the man had to say. Soon another man climbed onto the platform, took the microphone and shared his story about how God had helped him in his business that week.

This isn't going to end well. Where's the exit?

As my grandfather stood and waited, he began to understand what God was doing in the park that day. At the end of the afternoon, six people had dedicated their lives to the Lord accepting Jesus Christ as their personal Savior.

Demos Shakarian was standing in a vacant lot helping other people.

This was the first of many Sunday afternoons in the vacant lot across from Lincoln Park. The weekly Sunday afternoon meetings continued for three full months. By the end of those three months, almost everyone with whom Grandfather worked or conducted business with had come by to see him.

The news was out! People did view him differently now, but not in the way he feared. Conversely, they had a *greater* respect for him. After working six long days a week, Demos Shakarian was standing in a vacant lot helping other people. One of the many things that always stood out to me hearing this story was the role my grandmother played in it.

"I remember your grandfather with great delight because Demos always brought joy and a fresh anointing to every meeting I ever attended. My husband and I were married in 1954, and we became very active in his ministry. It was always refreshing to us spiritually to be a part of it. We would go to the monthly meetings on the first Saturday of each month. My husband would always say God spoke to him in a profound way during those times. It was a special time for him.

We were also able to attend some of Demos' overseas meetings. I recall fondly those in Finland and Sweden. I also recall fondly the various businessmen from all walks of life and how they would be so touched and transformed by the power of the Holy Spirit. Men from all over the world from various backgrounds coming together for a single purpose: To glorify God.

I thank God for your grandparents. They had such a vision and a passion for the power of the Holy Spirit, which literally shook the world!

Their faithfulness and vision continues on to this day. How blessed you are Cynthia, to be walking in a generational blessing!"

— **Marilyn Hickey** • President / Marilyn Hickey Ministries

CHAPTER NINE

Knott's Berry Farm Chicken Dinner

"*S*ometimes you can get so busy
with what you're expected to do,
you can easily miss
what you were born to do!"
— Cynthia Shakarian

I believe this fits the life of Grandfather. This could have so easily happened to him if he had not been so in tune with what was in his heart. He was already successful and extremely busy with the growing dairy business. I'm so thankful he stepped out to reach beyond the fences of his expanding dairy farm, to help change and impact the lives of people across the globe.

By doing this and listening to his heart, he stepped into his true calling and purpose!

As the summer ended, my grandfather took a break from his Sunday meetings in the vacant lot. Many of the surrounding churches were happy about this decision. They were more accustomed to seeing "Youth Meetings" in the park, instead of adults. They voiced their concerns to my grandparents, but thankfully my grandparents were listening to God.

The weather was cooling off, and the thriving family business required more of Grandfather's time. He had new ideas for marketing and wanted to expand the dairies to other locations, so he worked from early morning to late at night.

As springtime approached, my grandparents began talking about reviving the Sunday afternoon meetings. They decided to hold additional services and considered setting up an extremely large Tent so meetings could be held every evening, regardless of the weather. They discussed using the empty lot owned by the Armenian Church they attended in Los Angeles. Grandfather approached the elders to ask permission to use the lot. But after speaking with them, he quickly discovered they didn't have the same kind of enthusiasm.

They wanted to know all about the purpose of the meetings and the people who would be attending. Grandfather explained he intended to get Pentecostal churches in the area involved, as a way to bring them together.

He used the example of the Azusa Street Revival, which had brought unity to Los Angeles churches for a time. As the great Revival diminished, many of the churches which sprung up during this period eventually became isolated. Each group had so much to give its community. Unfortunately, many of these churches chose to keep the power of God within their church, rather than reaching out to their city. It seemed to be the religious culture at the time.

Grandfather was passionate about reversing this and to bring unity to the churches! He saw the need to get God's word out, as he noticed many businessmen had no idea such power and anointing of the Holy Spirit, was regularly experienced in churches all over Los Angeles.

"Although I never met Demos Shakarian, my life was impacted by his ministry. As a young believer who had just received the Baptism of the Holy Spirit, I was kicked out of my local church. So I was hungry for fellowship. His ministry was a place I could turn too. They always had great stories of God's power and demonstration.

Taking the gospel outside the walls of the church and bringing God's truths into the realm of business was powerful, effective, and appealing. I have endeavored to maintain that same focus in my own ministry, sharing how God's Kingdom impacts life where people live — in the marketplace!"

— **Gary Keesee** • Pastor, Host / Fixing the Money Thing

UNITING THE LOCAL CHURCHES

Despite Grandfather's pleas, the elders at the Armenian Pentecostal Church had their reservations. In conclusion, my grandfather finally said "If you let me use the land, I will take care of everything, including all financial responsibility. I will set up the event, clean it up afterward, and pay for it all." In the end, Isaac stepped forward to ask on behalf of Demos. The church relented and allowed him to use the lot. When Grandfather told this story, he always said it was his father's good reputation which saved the day.

As soon as he had permission to use the lot, the wheels were set in motion. The task was monumental. Grandfather could not believe how many city and county permits he needed. He thought holding meetings in a Tent would be easy, but he soon discovered this was going to be more challenging than he ever imagined.

In an effort to unite the local churches in his community, Grandfather picked five churches to get involved in helping with the meetings. He met with pastors from the *Foursquare Church,* the *Pentecostal Church of God,* the *Assemblies of God,* the *Armenian Pentecostal Church* and the *Pentecostal Holiness Church.* My grandfather was prepared to pay for all the expenses, but he had concerns about the churches being able to work together. That is until he came up with a plan.

He had such a heart to unite people of different faiths, colors, and beliefs.

He explained to the elders of these five churches if they worked together, and if the meetings generated a surplus of funds, he would deposit this money into a special account controlled and owned jointly by the church leaders. Then the five leaders could come together and decide how the funds should best be used.

The services in the Tent were to be held nightly for six weeks, and there would be costs involved such as; newspaper ads, flyers, radio announcements and equipment needed during the event. Because my grandfather had no experience in promoting public meetings, he followed the same advertising model he had used in his business. And it worked!

THE TENT MEETINGS

With everything in place, the evening meetings began that summer and continued for six weeks. My grandfather never considered himself to be a public speaker and had no intention of going through the anguish, the previous summer brought him. Instead, he decided to ask his second cousin, Harry Mushegan to do the preaching. Even though he was only in his early twenties, Harry was a great speaker. People enjoyed his teaching, which showed by the increase in attendance week after week.

My grandfather's younger sister, Florence, who was still in her late teens, agreed to sing in many of the services. Recently graduated from *Downey High,* Florence had a beautiful voice and was classically trained. She also liked the idea of helping her big brother whom she greatly admired. Eventually, the churches decided to work together. They came into agreement just as my grandfather had imagined.

No one ever made a big appeal for donations, yet they received a free-will offering each evening during the six weeks of services. The offerings increased night after night, just like the crowd and it was sufficient to pay for all of the promotional expenses. By the time the six weeks had passed all the costs had been covered, and money was left over. It was put in a special account for the five churches to control, as Grandfather promised. This turned into a double blessing. Now, these churches had to *talk and agree* on how to disburse the funds from *their joint account.* Brilliant! My grandfather's desire was for their newfound skill of communicating and working together to continue. Truly this had to be a God inspired idea!

The cooperation Grandfather saw among the five churches during the Tent meetings only intensified his desire, to bring together the pastors of different churches and denominations. He believed deep in his heart it could be done. Through the years, this was a theme I continually heard when others spoke about my grandfather. He had such a heart to unite people of different faiths, colors, and beliefs.

AIMEE SEMPLE MCPHERSON

In one of Grandfather's Tent meetings, a pastor who was skeptical of the Holy Spirit named Dr. Price, planned on attending to hear Aimee Semple McPherson speak. That my grandfather had a woman as the main guest speaker, was a big deal at that time because no one wanted to accept a woman preacher. One thing about my Bobby, he was open and flexible to how the Holy Spirit was moving. He would say, "Though God always stays the same, He is always doing something new. One thing is for sure; you cannot put God in a box. It is essential to have our hearts and our minds open to how the Spirit is flowing."

Years later, Dr. Price would confess to Grandfather that he had decided to attend the meeting for the purpose of taking notes to warn his congregation. He didn't believe in the Pentecostal experience being spoken about by Aimee Semple McPherson.

When she heard about his plan, she instructed to have Dr. Price sit on the stage next to the piano. She knew anyone who sat there was touched powerfully by the Holy Spirit. He was no exception. About midway through the service, Dr. Price knelt as he wept in God's presence. In that Tent meeting with Aimee Semple McPherson preaching, the Holy Spirit became real to him. The ministry of Dr. Charles Price was never the same after that night. He would see amazing miracles of healing in his meetings on a regular basis.

Sometime later upon meeting my grandfather, a deep friendship developed between them. They both experienced the power of the Holy Spirit in their lives, spiritually and professionally. Even how their paths first crossed was proven to be vital.

FLORENCE NEEDS A MIRACLE

My grandfather was in his office when Grandmother called him with the devastating news. His younger sister, Florence was driving early that morning when a truck smashed into her car. Though the air had been thick with fog that particular morning, my Bobby still wondered *"How could this have happened!"* Racing to the hospital, Grandmother met him at Downey Hospital along with his distraught father Isaac and many other family members. The news was not good. He was told the street she was driving on was in the middle of a repair. So when she was thrown from her car, she landed on extremely hot asphalt the road workers were pouring on the street.

Even before my grandfather entered her room, he could hear her groaning in pain. At that moment all my grandfather wanted for his sister was to be out of pain. Which is what he prayed continuously and it seemed to work. As he prayed her groaning subsided. He was required to wear a cap, gown, and booties whenever he got near his sister to keep her room sterile. The doctors said nothing seems to be helping her except when her big brother is in the room praying.

Her pelvis had been crushed, but the doctors could not fix her broken bones because of the extreme burns she had suffered. News spread of what happened to Florence, and immediately all the members of the church in East Los Angeles agreed to go on a one-day total fast; to pray God would completely heal her. Later that night my grandfather felt led to meet a man he had been hearing about for months. He was experiencing tremendous healings in his meetings. His name was Dr. Charles Price.

That evening my grandfather went to where Dr. Price was holding a meeting. As Grandfather tried to approach the front podium so he could talk to him, the crowds continued to cut in front of him. But my grandfather was determined as he remembered the moans of his sister. Just as Dr. Price was about to leave

Grandfather saw an opening and took it. "Dr. Price!" He called out talking as fast as he could; "My name is Demos Shakarian, and my sister is at the hospital in desperate need of a healing. Will you please come and pray for her?"

My Bobby was surprised by what happened next. Dr. Price, in a remarkably calm voice and appearing not to be in a rush said, "Don't worry, your sister will be just fine. In fact, she will be healed tonight. Yes, let's go see her now." *Healed tonight? Obviously, he does not realize how badly she is injured,* Grandfather thought. Seeing the surprised look on Grandfather's face, he went on to tell him about another recent miracle. It was the reason why he was so sure his sister would be healed immediately.

THE WARM BANKET EXPERIENCE

Dr. Price explained how he prayed for a woman who had been paralyzed for ten years. He knew that night she would be healed because every time he walked near her 'a warm, thick blanket' seemed to wrap around his shoulders. Dr. Price described it as an unusual sensation, *having comforting warmth with a heavy presence surrounding it.*

Well, now he had my Bobby's complete attention, as my grandfather had experienced the same supernatural feeling at thirteen years old. Suddenly, my Bobby agreed. Yes, his sister would be healed that night. But Dr. Price wasn't finished, he said as soon as he heard my Bobby's voice, that same 'warm blanket' came over his shoulders. Dr. Price said, "We are going to experience another miracle tonight! God is doing something."

Arriving at the hospital, Dr. Price anointed Florence with

oil he had brought with him. He thanked the Lord for healing Florence. As he was praising God, suddenly Florence started to move around, even though she had wires and tubes attached to her. When she suddenly whispered to her brother, "I'm healed, I know Jesus healed me!"

All the doctors confirmed her healing the next day after new x-rays were taken. They could not believe what they saw, no broken bones, even her pelvis was no longer broken. In fact, her left pelvis matched her right pelvis exactly, though her left pelvis had been crushed. Her burns were still healing, but now she was recovering because there was nothing else wrong with her. One month later, she left the hospital after the wounds healed knowing God had miraculously touched her. Dr. Price and my grandfather would become life-long friends after this first encounter.

LOVE FOR THE MILITARY

Many changes had come to the United States. Pearl Harbor had been attacked, and the war was continuing in other parts of the world. Almost overnight, Los Angeles became a hub of defense-related activity. The roads were jammed with army trucks. A significant influx of soldiers and military personnel had come to the Los Angeles area around 1941.

My grandfather had not been drafted into the war. Dairy farmers were needed in the United States, so they were omitted from the draft. Still, he had an overwhelming love and respect for the military. During this time, he was directed by the Lord to hold a Tent meeting specifically for the military and their families. He discussed this with my grandmother, who was also very enthusiastic about the idea. Though there was one significant point, they disagreed on. Who would be the speaker? This was very unusual as they normally agreed.

> *A man who has been blessed with success needs God as much as anyone else.*

Grandfather thought Dr. Price would be a great speaker for the event. My grandmother felt strongly that although Dr. Price was an incredible speaker, a younger person would be better for this particular meeting. "Someone," my Momie continued, "who the soldiers could better relate too."

Excited to have the meeting, he decided to go ahead and try to set it up with Dr. Price speaking. Grandfather was also working on obtaining permission for the meeting from military personnel. It appeared one obstacle after another kept the meeting from coming together. In the meantime, life got in the way! The needs of the Dairies diverted his attention. Before he knew it, this opportunity passed him by.

My grandfather was disappointed in himself, and this disappointment stayed with him. This was especially because he regarded the military so highly and had such love and respect for their sacrifice. The look on his face, when he talked about this missed opportunity has stuck with me. He said he missed God on the timing and didn't move when the Lord directed him. This event etched a note in my mind: *"Move when God is leading you to do so. Go with His timing, and not my own!* When God says "Now," he means "Now." Later in my own life, I would learn that valuable lesson ... the hard way! I should have paid better attention to my Bobby's life-lesson.

Grandfather was able to honor the military years later when he regularly held "Military Breakfasts" at his conventions. There, many servicemen gathered from all branches of the military including Generals, Colonels, and every rank in between. They shared incredible stories of bravery and God's protection in the face of danger.

BRINGING BUSINESSMEN TOGETHER

Over lunch one afternoon, Grandfather was talking with Dr. Price about how many of his friends had been drafted. "It seems all the men have been taken out of the city." Dr. Price corrected him, "The city is overrun with soldiers," he told my grandfather. Startled by his words, Grandfather questioned what Dr. Price was saying, "But the Tent meetings are always filled with more women than men." "Yes," said Dr. Price, who was a bit amused. "There seem to be more women attending church services too." Until my grandparents started holding Tent meetings, my grandfather didn't realize it was primarily women who attended church. They outnumbered the men, 10 to 1. A man who has been blessed with success needs God as much as anyone else. Grandfather thought about how he could solve this problem.

Dr. Price told Grandfather that many businessmen came to him asking business questions. He felt qualified to counsel them in spiritual matters only. As he excitedly explained to my grandfather, "Perhaps you could discuss business with these men. A businessman can relate to another businessman." Several weeks later, during one of their regular get-togethers, Dr. Price prophesied to my grandfather, *he would see important events soon.* Dr. Price said, "God is going to pour out His Spirit upon the whole earth and all flesh. Demos, you are going to play a significant role and be a big part in all of this coming to pass!"

CAROLYN

My grandmother gave birth to their third child Carolyn, on November 1, 1944. My grandparents purchased the most beautiful clothes for their new little bundle from heaven. She also received wonderful gifts for her baby girl from many in the Armenian community.

Carolyn was special to my grandparents from the moment she was born. She always had a radiant glow about her. As the community flocked to the house to meet the new baby and bring her gifts, my grandparents began to notice everyone commenting on Carolyn's happy and loving nature. The darling twinkle in her eye was captivating.

Then the unthinkable happened that following March. A strong strain of influenza hit Los Angeles. Baby Carolyn who was only five months old, became ill very quickly. She was diagnosed with pneumonia in both lungs. Suddenly only hours after the diagnosis she was gone, joining Great-great-grandfather Demos in Heaven.

Devastated by this sudden and tragic event, my grandmother, in particular, had a hard time even looking at another baby. Yet, she and my grandfather did what they always did. They turned to God and to prayer. For weeks my grandparents were flooded with love from the community, though it seemed to bring little comfort. Until an incredible source of peace came one afternoon when friends stopped by my grandparents' home. The friends were a few women from church who were known to be incredibly strong in the gifts of the Holy Spirit. They told my grandparents when they walked in they saw angels all over their home. In fact, the women continued, the house was filled with them! Though still devastated, this brought my grandparents' comfort knowing God had not forgotten them. He had sent angels to surround them and restore peace during this heartbreaking time.

My grandfather turned to spending additional time on his knees in prayer, realizing he needed to surrender even more of his daily life to God. "Though I have organized Tent meetings and desired to be your servant, You have not been my priority. Now Lord, from this day forward You will no longer be *a priority*, but *THE priority* Lord Jesus."

THE SHRINE AUDITORIUM

In the summer of 1945, my grandfather began to think about getting churches in the area together again. This time, however, his vision expanded as he prayed. *The Youth* in the churches wanted an event of their own and asked my grandfather to spearhead it. He gathered a group of men to discuss the event when it was suggested they would need to raise $300. My grandfather said "We must believe for more. The goal should be at least $3,000."

The people smiled knowing that was *Grandfather's way*! He was a man who always thought bigger!

He suggested using the "Shrine Auditorium," a Los Angeles historic landmark. Many thought this venue was unattainable. In later years, it became the site of the Academy Awards, the Grammy Awards, the American Music Awards, and many other events.

A couple of summers ago this idea would have seemed ridiculous. Renting the *Shrine Auditorium* would be very expensive. There would be promotional expenses such as radio advertising, posters, and flyers. This would double or triple the costs. Also lighting, sound, parking, and everything else connected to holding an event at such a large venue would need to be considered. Quickly realizing the pastors of the Pentecostal churches were not the answer for sponsoring such an event, Grandfather thought, *What about businessmen?*

KNOTT'S BERRY FARM

Reverting to his roots Grandfather knew that in business, the most important decisions are made around the table enjoying good food together. He decided to ask pastors' to invite 100 business men to a chicken dinner, and not just any chicken dinner. This one would be held at Knott's Berry Farm, an amusement park famous for its delicious fried chicken.

Once again most of the pastors were hesitant, but Bobby had a lot of patience. They eventually came up with the names of 100 business people. Grandfather invited all of them including their spouses to be his guests for a chicken dinner. The details were finalized and when the date arrived the dining room at *Knott's Berry Farm* was filled. He and Grandmother were seated so they could see everyone in the room.

As I looked into all the faces in the room, an amazing thought came to me, Grandfather would tell me. "What if I asked five or six of them to come up to the front and tell how the Lord has impacted their life, or how their life and family have benefited from attending church together?" He especially wanted to hear from men who were successful in their businesses because they were a rare sight in the church. Plus, a few businessmen speaking to a room filled with other businessmen, could be an inspiration to those who did not know the Lord personally!

THE SHINING SPOTLIGHT

As my Bobby pondered this, his eyes fell upon a tall man dressed in a blue three-piece suit. Suddenly, the man's face appeared to light up. This was the same kind of spotlight that had shined on the livestock which my grandfather purchased, especially "Pabst Leader." He knew this would be the first man he would invite to speak. Grandfather waited anxiously for the meal to end. As soon as he had an opportunity, he walked to the microphone and motioned for the tall man to come to the front of the room.

The man looked like a deer caught in headlights, but he slowly rose to his feet and walked to the microphone. Would you be so kind as to share with everyone what the Lord means to you?" Grandfather asked him. A smile spread across the man's face. "It's funny you should ask," he began by saying. "The Lord has been so good to my family, particularly in recent months." The man told the crowd how God had miraculously turned his failing business around to a thriving company. As he ended, he shared how he thanked the Lord every day for answering his prayers.

Businessmen speaking to businessmen could be an inspiration!

Silence fell across the dining room as the businessmen contemplated the joyful words the man shared. As he returned to his seat, Grandfather looked across the room and saw a bright light shining on another businessman's face.

He too had a wonderful testimony to share with the group. Grandfather said this went on and on with one person after another, sharing stories of healing, families restored, and businesses miraculously flourishing.

An hour and a half later, my Bobby ended the evening with his own words. He told the crowd, they had heard about God's love as told from one businessman to another. Everyone thought they were going to hear my grandfather give a big appeal to raise money. What they heard instead were inspirational stories of real events about how God was changing people's lives.

He told the crowd his desire to spread God's good news to as many people as they could. Further explaining if he could raise enough money, this would be done at the *Shrine Auditorium* so thousands could hear about God's power. As my grandfather finished speaking, people began rushing to place money on his table. Some gave cash while others wrote checks, and by the end of the evening, he had raised $6,200.

This was enough to hold two events! In the 1940s, that amount of money could have purchased one new home, five or six new automobiles, or the equivalent of two men's yearly wage.

THE YOUTH RALLY

Grandfather knew he was led in the way he conducted the meeting and called upon the men one by one. He instinctively knew he would follow this pattern in the future. As he fell asleep, he dreamed of what would happen if businessmen started to encourage other businessmen about the things of God. Though he saw himself as someone who did not speak in front of large groups of people, he trusted that God saw something in him, he did not see in himself. Immediately, he began preparing for the event at the *Shrine Auditorium*, again using his experience in promoting his business as a model to follow.

The excitement was rapidly building the night of the *Youth Rally*. It was March 29, 1948. The Shrine Auditorium reached its maximum capacity quickly. Many others were trying to find a seat, but there was none to be had. R.W. Culpepper a young evangelist was among the huge gathering standing outside hoping to get in. While waiting, he began praying for a teenage boy standing next to him who asked for prayer. As he did, God's power came over the entire crowd like a glorious wave. Suddenly the large crowd outside, one by one, started singing and praising the Lord.

News traveled quickly about Culpepper and the move of God which had settled amongst the huge crowd outside. Suddenly the presence of God came upon everyone inside as well!

> "Demos Shakarian was nothing less than a walking legend. I first encountered him when I was only eight years old at a Diner in Anaheim, California. He was gracious, loving and above all kind.
>
> In the world of Christianity, he is one of the greatest leaders in the last 100 years. He was a pioneer who blazed new trails where others could follow."
>
> — **Tim Storey** • Interviewed by Oprah Winfrey / OWN's *Super Soul Sunday* / Speaker

CHAPTER TEN

A Night At The Hollywood Bowl

✦

Through the years, I observed as Grandfather would pick the best and most appealing places to hold his meetings. Time and time again, his methods proved him right. I believe this was another Divine insight he seemed to have.

Now turning his attention to the second event, he remembered the previous year with his success of uniting five churches. He pondered, *What would happen if all of the three-hundred Pentecostal churches in the Los Angeles area came together in one place?* The first venue which came to Grandfather's mind big enough to hold a crowd of that size was the "Hollywood Bowl," a landmark amphitheater.

MONDAY NIGHT AT THE BOWL

That Monday night at the *Hollywood Bowl* on September 27, 1948, was more than a success. The place was packed and every seat was taken. There were 22,000 people seated, with thousands more standing in the aisles.

On this warm autumn night at the outdoor amphitheater, the stars were shining brightly. The air was charged with antic-ipation. As everyone entered the *Hollywood Bowl,* they were given candles. Grandfather walked across the stage, taking the

If each of us shares the love of God with others, we can light up the world!

microphone. He asked all participants to light their candles.

What a beautiful sight it must have been! More than 20,000 candles flickering in the dark. Then Grandfather boldly proclaimed, "Just as one candle cannot light up the *Hollywood Bowl* but with everyone together, there is light. So too goes the Word of God."

"It's impossible to accurately assess the worldwide influence of Demos Shakarian. Like a happy, life-giving 'microorganism,' through most of this remarkable-though-humble man's life, everyone he touched was impacted with a love and generosity that defies description. On first impression, a genuine warmth and happy concern radiated from a smiling face and an inner Spirit, which can only be called Holy.

Demos knew businessmen on every level wielded much influence, but they were also tempted and harassed by this world's pressures in ways, which often bore them down. They were distracted from the ways their loving God would like to bless them. So Demos built an international organization which blessed and taught millions about their loving Heavenly Father and His Holy Spirit power.

I was fortunate to know Demos and call him friend and to participate in a number of his meetings. My father and I, at separate times, experienced and grew spiritually by our fellowship with Demos. That's why I say Demos' 'happy Holy Spirit influence' was so contagious. Only God in Heaven will reveal the millions which were affected . . . and continue to be!"

— **Pat Boone** • Singer, Actor / Second biggest charting artist of the 1950s behind Elvis Presley / Three Stars on the Hollywood Walk of Fame Music, Movies, and Television

My Bobby understood his purpose, but he was unaware of what was about to transpire. Soon he would ultimately ignite a spark and set the world on fire. He had held Tent meetings for seven summers and the ground-breaking *Hollywood Bowl* meeting. He continued his efforts encouraging churches to work together and sponsoring many great evangelists.

My grandfather was behind the scene, right where he felt comfortable.

Grandfather was behind the scene, which was right where he felt comfortable. Though that was about to change . . . in a big way!

"My wife and I became born-again in 1985 in Hollywood, California, when Jesus Christ got a hold of our lives. Up to that point, we were Hollywood entertainers dancing as a husband and wife pop-locking team, a form of urban dance in the industry.

After we were born again, we began to pursue the Lord and serve Him with our talents. During that time we heard of Demos' organization, and we attended the meetings. It was very powerful seeing people in Hollywood who loved Jesus. They were reaching out in a setting that wasn't 'churchy,' but it was very effective in impacting people who usually would not go to church.

His meetings made a powerful impact on my life and showed me you can be unique and different, and yet powerful in your witness in your own arena of life. To this day I am thankful and grateful for Demos Shakarian and the vision, to take the gospel to Hollywood and around the world!"

— Ruckins McKinley, D.D • Speaker, Author / "The Sound"

TRIALS IN THE MONTHS AHEAD

Though my grandfather felt great things would happen after the successful *Hollywood Bowl* meeting, the following year was a time of frustration and trials.

Rose and Demos lived next door to his parents, Isaac and Zarouhi. My grandfather often said how he loved spending time with his mom. Though I never met her, I can imagine her beautiful and positive spirit. She was forever an optimist, and she adored her husband Isaac and son, my grandfather Demos. She always wore a smile on her face. Grandfather loved being in her home because God's peace was tangible. Beyond that, she was a great source of inspiration and encouragement to him.

Soon Isaac's precious wife, and my great-grandmother, Zarouhi passed away at only fifty years of age, after a prolonged illness. My great-grandfather Isaac was devastated, as he deeply loved her. Though he was working long hours at the dairies, he was extremely lonely at home without her. Fortunately, my grandparents lived next door and were able to be very attentive. Additionally, so Isaac wouldn't be alone, my father, Richard started spending more time at my Great-Bobby's home. He greatly admired *his grandfather* Isaac, so this was welcomed time together. My Aunt Geri also adored time with her grandfather.

It became apparent my family was not the only ones who enjoyed spending time with Zarouhi. As attendance at her funeral was the largest Downey had ever seen. Everyone remembered her encouraging words and sunny disposition. The funeral was packed with not only leaders from the surrounding area but also many homeless people the family had helped. Especially those whom she had cooked for and shared her delicious meals.

At the same time, they were presented with disastrous news. The quarterly reports for the family's business showed the mill they had acquired, was facing an uphill battle. *Reliance Dairy* needed to consider making some major changes to preserve the company. With Grandfather's thoughts on the mill, seemingly out of nowhere the word "Fresno" started popping into his mind. Fresno is a town about two-hundred miles north of Los Angeles, but my grandfather did not know anyone there. So why did he keep thinking about Fresno?

In fact, my grandfather had been adamantly opposed to expanding his summer meetings beyond the Los Angeles area. He enjoyed strong relationships with several pastors in Los Angeles, all of whom cooperated with him. In another city far away he would not have that luxury.

When talking with my grandmother, he said, "Something strange is happening. I spent the whole drive home unable to think about anything except . . ." Before my grandfather could say the city name, my grandmother said, "Fresno?" Grandfather could not believe what he was hearing. He chuckled. After all, it had happened many times before. "God must be up to something," he said to Grandmother.

Yet, they knew by now to rely on God for the next step because He always came through. First, they were given the name of a pastor in Fresno whom my grandfather telephoned immediately. Grandfather shared the experience he had with the Los Angeles Tent meetings. He asked the pastor if he would consider holding such meetings in Fresno. The pastor wanted to think about it, promising to call back in a few days.

Grandfather wasn't sure what would come of this conversation, but he knew God was calling him to Fresno for a purpose. He believed the pastor would also hear from God. The call came a few days later. The pastor was on board!

Within a matter of weeks, my grandfather drove to Fresno and hosted a steak dinner for the pastor, along with 33 other Fresno-area pastors and their wives. Though the Fresno pastors were not entirely sold on the idea, Grandfather used the same model for the Fresno dinner that he used at the *Knotts Berry Farm* meeting. Grandfather always said that offering good food is one way to ensure a great turnout. I guess what Grandfather used to say is true. Feed the body and people will come… then you can feed their soul!

HEY, WHAT'S IN IT FOR YOU?

As soon as the dinner was finished, my grandfather began to share what happened in Los Angeles during the summer Tent meetings. He explained how thousands of people had come to know Jesus Christ as their Lord and Savior. As Grandfather continued to speak, he looked at the faces of everyone seated around the tables. They were all staring back at him with no expression. The silence was so loud; you could hear the crickets outside!

Grandfather paused for a moment to collect his thoughts, when one man speaking in a loud voice said, "What do you get out of it, Mr. Shakarian?" Startled by the question at first but after reflecting a moment, he realized a good pastor *should* be watchful over the well-being of the people in his congregation.

"Thank you for asking," my Bobby said before explaining further. "I think it is important everyone knows the answer to that vital question before committing. First of all, I do not take a salary from the meetings. I pay all my own expenses. In this case, my expenses would include the relocation of my family. We would live here for the duration of the meetings. Any donations would be used to pay for only the cost of the meetings, including advertising, audio equipment, and the like. If there are remaining funds after these costs, I will deposit it into a joint bank account controlled by the churches who participate in the meetings. They can then decide how to best use the funds."

It now appeared to my grandfather he had their attention, so he continued. "If the offerings do not cover the meetings expenses, I will pay the difference out of my pocket. Deficits will never be your responsibility. Instead, I will be completely financially responsible for the event. In other words, the churches would be sponsoring this outreach with no liability."

To lighten the mood, Grandfather playfully bent his arm looking down the sleeve of his suit coat saying, "Nope, no tricks up my sleeve here!" The pastors all broke into laughter and now with smiles on their faces; they listened more intently.

FINDING HIS SPECIAL TALENT

Sir, you asked what I get out of it, so let me explain. I believe everyone has a God-given talent which is to be used for His glory. I believe if we use our special gift, we will find inner peace which can come only from God. On the other hand, if we fail to use our unique talents we will fail to fulfill our God-given purpose in life.

I've found my special job. It's to encourage people and show them the fullness of God's love, uniting them and helping to bring out the best in them. God has put your city on my heart, and I want to fulfill my purpose by helping in every aspect of this initiative.

Then he read 1 Corinthians 12:4-14 from his Bible which says:

4 There are different kinds of spiritual gifts, but the same Spirit is the source of them all. 5 There are different kinds of working, but in all of them and in everyone it is the same God at work.

7 Now to each one the manifestation of the Spirit is given for the common good. 8 To one there is given through the Spirit a message of wisdom, to another a message of knowledge by means of the same Spirit, 9 to another faith by the same Spirit, to another gifts of healing by that one Spirit, 10 to another miraculous powers, to another prophecy, to another distinguishing between spirits, to another speaking in different kinds of tongues, and to still another the interpretation of tongues.11 All these are the work of one and the same Spirit, and he distributes them to each one, just as he determines.

12 Just as a body, though one, has many parts, but all its many parts form one body, so it is with Christ. 13 For we were all baptized by one Spirit so as to form one body—whether Jews or Gentiles, slave or free—and we were all given the one Spirit to drink. 14 Even so the body is not made up of one part but of many.

When my grandfather stopped talking, the silence was so thick you could have heard a pin drop. At that moment, anyone originally questioning Grandfather's motives was now on board, realizing God indeed called this man.

After that dinner, Grandfather and the pastors began to plan for the meetings. They worked together, and before they knew it, they had secured an auditorium, purchased advertising and enrolled volunteers. The pastors suggested the meetings be held in the month of October because summers in Fresno were incredibly hot. My grandparents soon found a suitable place to rent and made their plans to spend two months there. They wanted to arrive ahead of the five-week meetings and stay long enough to tie-up all the administrative details.

Before leaving for Fresno, Grandfather went to the recently acquired mill, which was of great concern to him financially. He planned to finish some last minute business before leaving town the next morning. When he arrived at the mill, he was met with devastating news about grain commodities and losses. The grain prices grew even worse the following day. The downward trend continued. Beyond that, making a temporary move was no small feat.

HIS FRESNO EXPERIENCE

The items they needed to bring with them had multiplied, as they had been blessed with another son. As far back as anyone could remember, no Shakarian man had more than one son, and Grandfather now had two!

My grandparents were thrilled about their new baby boy. In addition to my father Richard and his sister Geri, they now had another little boy named Steve, who was born on July 12, 1947. Grandmother wanted to make sure she had everything needed for her baby. The truck couldn't fit one more item.

With the truck on its way up to Fresno, Grandfather turned his attention back to the mill and the pending financial disaster. Then one of his employees said something which made my grandfather stop and ponder. "I know your trip will mean a lot to the people of Fresno, but how can you even think about leaving now with the losses going on at the mill?" Instead of responding, my grandfather thought for a moment. He remembered his commitment to the Lord. When his infant daughter had passed, he had fallen to his knees promising God *HE would be Grandfather's priority.* As he took a moment, my Bobby heard no instruction from God to change the plan. "I will stay in touch and follow up by phone," he replied to his concerned employee before leaving. And off he went!

This wasn't an easy choice. My grandparents, Aunt Geri, little Steve and his baby-nurse, Mrs. Newman drove the two-hundred miles to Fresno. My dad Richard stayed in Downey with my great-grandfather Isaac. While driving, Grandfather wondered why the Lord would have him leave, when the falling grain prices could so quickly destroy the family business. But even as his mind wandered, he kept his eyes on the highway and continued toward Fresno.

Later that afternoon, upon arriving at the rented house the challenges continued. While unpacking, my grandmother suddenly noticed her beautiful diamond engagement watch, which my grandfather had placed on her wrist so many years ago, had fallen off. She couldn't find it anywhere. Her watch had tremendous sentimental meaning to her. *How could this happen,* she wondered. She, my grandfather and Mrs. Newman searched every nook and cranny, going through all the boxes they had just unpacked. It was nowhere to be found. Then while the frantic search was continuing, suddenly baby Steve came down with a fever and became very ill. Grandmother called a local doctor, but Steve's temperature continued to rise. My grandparents were overwhelmed with everything going on and turned to prayer.

In faith, my grandfather called his father and asked Isaac to let the church know prayers for the baby were needed. My grandparents were up all night along with Mrs. Newman caring for their son. Their minds constantly thinking of baby Carolyn's fate. But by morning still under a doctor's care, baby Steve's health grew worse. My grandfather also received bad news from the mill. There were even greater losses.

Grandfather tried to make sense out of what was happening, stopping regularly to pray. His mind was occupied with thoughts of his infant son, so he continued asking God to confirm if coming to Fresno was His idea. All day long, he heard the same nagging, critical voice. *Take your family and go back to Los Angeles,* this voice told him. *Leave Fresno!*

In prayer the next morning, my grandfather realized he recognized the voice. "Rose! Rose!" he said, "It is not the voice of the Lord! This voice lacks God's presence. I should not listen to this voice! If this voice is telling us to call off the meetings here in Fresno, it must mean something great is going to happen!" "God is in this!" he told my grandmother. Momie, who was sleep-deprived and greatly concerned for her son, wiped her eyes. Right there and then my grandparents in faith, began to thank the Lord for being with them and healing their infant son, even though there was still no change in baby Steve's fever.

WILLIAM BRANHAM & KELSO GLOVER

And with that announcement, Grandfather got everything ready to begin the event, which was to be held every night from October 10th thru October 31st. The opening speaker was Kelso Glover followed by William Branham. His services were always packed with miracles and healing. By the time the last Sunday afternoon meeting was beginning, the 35,000 seat auditorium was overflowing. Thousands more stood along the walls and in the aisles. Dismissal time came and went, but people continued to praise God and worship Him.

It was incredible! The Holy Spirit had taken over the meetings. The power of God was so thick that Glover literally 'felt' His presence! Miracles began unfolding right in front of the thousands of attendees. It was almost midnight before the service came to an end. Illnesses had been cured, and people had dedicated their lives to the Lord.

The power of God was so thick Glover literally 'felt' His presence!

Grandfather was full of joy, thankful he continued with the meetings as God had directed him. He was even more thankful; baby Steve received his healing and was no longer sick! Before leaving Fresno, everything came full circle. Grandmother also miraculously found her missing treasured watch at the bottom of one of the boxes.

THE MILL

The miracles kept coming even after my grandfather returned to Los Angeles. There was a cash buyer for the milling business, named Mr. Weinberg. He was eager to make the purchase because he said *God told him to buy it*. So although he was anxious to present his offer, he had to wait 10 days for Grandfather to arrive back in Downey. He was surprised Grandfather stayed in Fresno so long, knowing he had an all-cash buyer for the failing mill waiting for him.

Upon Grandfather's return, the discussions began. Unfortunately, negotiations fell apart. He decided not to buy the mill because they were $25,000 apart in the price. But then a miracle happened. God spoke to Mr. Weinberg, waking him up in the night, telling him; *he was to buy the mill – at the price which was asked.* The next morning, he met with Great-Bobby Isaac and Grandfather for breakfast, sealing the deal with a handshake. He agreed to buy the mill at their asking price of over $500,000.

My Bobby put God's business first in Fresno, and God took care of everything else. God also blessed Mr. Weinberg for obeying the voice of the Lord. The mill would become very successful because Mr. Weinberg listened to God.

After months of frustration and turmoil, every circumstance turned around. God's faithfulness was demonstrated in every situation. Grandfather believed God was preparing him for something more, especially after this time of intense training. He wondered what was in-store for him next. As *God would use ordinary men with ordinary jobs, people in businesses, to spread His love.* he continued to seek God for direction, the words of his friend Charles Price came to his mind. He had told my grandfather; he believed God would use ordinary men with ordinary jobs, people in businesses, shops, factories, and offices, to spread His love.

Seeking direction, Grandfather began to think bigger and dream bigger. He would ask himself, *What would happen if this same thing occurred in other places besides California? What if hundreds or even thousands of men in all kinds of businesses, came together to glorify God and spread the Good News all over the world?*

WISE WORDS FROM KATHRYN KUHLMAN

The amazing evangelist Kathryn Kuhlman was among those who ministered in some of my Bobby's early meetings. I believe this quotation by her defines why God used my grandfather in such a unique and powerful way. "The Heavenly Father does not ask for golden vessels," she said. "He does not ask for silver vessels. God asks for yielded vessels, those who will submit *their will* to the will of the Father. The greatest human attainment in the world is for a life to be surrendered to Him, that the name of God be glorified through their life."

This was my grandfather – a yielded vessel who submitted his will, to the will of his Heavenly Father. In particular when it had to do with anything which might hinder the Spirit and God's anointing over his organization. This included when a decision had to be made, that was not a popular decision to make. He was determined above everything else to complete the purpose of why he was on this earth ... without compromise.

BILLY GRAHAM,
ORAL ROBERTS, KENNETH HAGIN...

My grandparents continued to sponsor evangelists in Los Angeles each summer. This included many men and women of God such as Billy Graham, Oral Roberts, and Dr. Charles Price. In later years this group grew to include Kathryn Kuhlman, Kenneth Hagin, Sr. and many others. Every year the meetings increased in size and became more successful than the previous year.

"I had the privilege of meeting and fellowshipping with Demos Shakarian after I got out of the United States Army in 1965. For many years, my dad, Kenneth E. Hagin, Sr. was involved with Demos in his ministry. My dad esteemed Demos Shakarian very highly. I can recall many times Demos would call my dad and ask him to pray about different matters. They had a very close relationship.

Grandfather began to think bigger and dream bigger!

During many of Demos' World Conventions, he would look down the head table and say, 'Brother Hagin, I believe you have something.' Dad would say, 'Yes, I do,' and then go up and share. Demos once told Dad, 'Different ones can teach on faith and healing, but you're the best one at teaching on the Holy Spirit.' I can remember in one meeting watching as many as four-hundred people stand and receive the Holy Spirit all at once.

I know my dad, Kenneth E. Hagin, Sr. was glad to call Demos Shakarian his friend!"

— Kenneth W. Hagin, Jr. • Rhema Ministries,
Kenneth Hagin Ministries

CHAPTER ELEVEN

Breakfast at Clifton's Cafeteria

My Bobby made a point to tell me how important it was to listen to that still small voice inside you. Sometimes it's a seed being planted and deeply rooted in your soul for greater things you're destined to do in your life.

Although he was thrilled with sponsoring meetings, restlessness began to take hold of him. Deep inside he could not shake it off, nor did he want too.

He believed something new was coming and he was prepared to move in the direction the Holy Spirit was leading him. Though for now, he was waiting for a fuller understanding of just what this new direction would be!

GREAT-GRANDFATHER ISAAC'S
DREAM REALIZED

As the early 1940s were drawing to a close, Great-Bobby's "start-up herd" of three cows had grown to three-thousand. The growth in his business continued until they owned 5,000 Holstein cows.

Reliance Dairy had indeed become 'the largest privately owned dairy in the world.' A DREAM COME TRUE!

"Everyone has a dream, but there are those who believe their dreams are really God's ideas. Demos Shakarian was such a man. Bearing the fruit of believing God, he created a unique platform for spreading the gospel.

Cynthia Shakarian carries a prophetic passion for the continuation of her grandfather's vision. God bless Demos Shakarian for his faithfulness!"

— Gary Zamora • Pastor / Gary Zamora Ministries

Since he was thirteen years old, my grandfather had been asking the Lord one question, "What is the unique talent I have been given to do in this world?" One morning in prayer the answer came to him. The Bible talks about prophets, teachers of the Word, and many other positions.

> *"What is the unique talent I have been given to do?"*

My grandfather finally received the answer to his question. He knew what his special purpose was. He was a "helper and an encourager," bringing businessmen together giving them the opportunity to know the love of God. This included helping them to discover the fullness and the power of *all* of God's Spiritual gifts!

A VISIONARY

In the fall of the early 1950s, my grandfather organized Oral Roberts' city-wide meetings in Los Angeles. The meetings lasted for sixteen days and were the largest gatherings Los Angeles had ever experienced. Over 200,000 people attended.

One afternoon my grandfather and Oral Roberts were having coffee together. Grandfather mentioned how wonderful the services were and how much he loved putting all the details of the meetings together. "But I feel I am supposed to be doing something else," he told him.

"Tell me more," encouraged Oral Roberts. "What has God put on your heart to do?"

Looking down while stirring his coffee, my Bobby said, "I don't have all of the details yet. What I know for certain, is it involves ordinary businessmen. Those who know the Lord and love Him, but who have not stepped out in faith and shared their experience with other people in their field of business."

Oral Roberts was intrigued. Pushing his pie away, he crossed his arms and listened intently as he asked for more information. My grandfather explained how it had always bothered him, that men who became successful in business often stopped going to church. Further explaining that he wanted to see businessmen share with other businessmen, about how they experienced the life-changing power of God in their lives.

Grandfather finally received the answer to his question, he knew his special purpose. He was a "helper and an encourager."

Grandfather told his friend, "I know some businessmen will not go to church and listen to a preacher, but they will listen to other like-minded people in business if they were able to speak in a familiar and comfortable environment. Maybe like a restaurant or hotel ballroom. Can you imagine, we could have thousands of chapters meeting in every city of America, or better yet in every city around the world!"

As Oral Roberts sipped his coffee curiosity took over and he said, "Does this organization have a name?"

My Bobby knew exactly how to answer him. God had already given him the name during a night of prayer. "It will be worldwide, so the group will be called Full Gospel Business Men's Fellowship International (FGBMFI)."

"Wow! That's quite a long name." Oral exclaimed.

My grandfather continued with his explanation, "Ordinary businessmen will be able to share what God has done in their lives. It will not be a church meeting, but rather a group of men who get together because they want to encourage each other and have fellowship with one another."

"I want you to know two things," Oral Roberts said. "First, I can feel the Lord is all over this. Secondly, I'm with you!"

"That's good," my grandfather proclaimed, "because I am going to invite businessmen from all around Los Angeles to a Saturday morning breakfast meeting. I'd like you to be our first guest speaker!"

> "The first memories I have of Demos and the Shakarian family, are the times we would visit the family home in Downey, California. I especially remember the rice pilaf Rose would make. It was delicious! I'll never forget the day my father spoke at the first men's breakfast at Clifton's Cafeteria. I was privileged to attend many conferences where my dad was the main speaker.
>
> In addition to knowing Demos Shakarian as a teenager, I traveled with my dad to many of Demos' conventions. I also knew him from his involvement as a member of the Board of Trustees of the Oral Roberts Evangelistic Association. As a teenager, I was with Demos, my dad, and the rest of the board when we broke ground to build Oral Roberts University in Tulsa, Oklahoma. Demos was a great help to my dad from the very beginning of ORU. I remember us all at the University groundbreaking and dedication in April 1967.

Some had tried to talk my dad out of putting a Prayer Tower in the center of the campus, but Demos insisted the Prayer Tower should be the focal point so everyone would understand from the beginning, that ORU was dedicated to God.

I also attended the dedication of 'The Shakarian Hall' on the campus of Oral Roberts University!"

— **Richard Roberts** • Son of Oral Roberts / Oral Roberts Ministries

THE SHAKARIAN HALL

It was a wonderful recognition when Oral Roberts, the Executive Committee, and the Board of Regents of Oral Roberts University, voted to honor my great-grandfather and my grandfather by naming the men's dormitory, "The Shakarian Hall." They wanted to show their gratitude for their significant contribution in helping to get ORU built. Though my Great-Bobby

Oral Roberts University honored Grandfather by naming the men's dormitory, "The Shakarian Hall."

Isaac was not there to see it; Grandfather was very honored and moved by this grand distinction.

At the Dedication of ORU in 1967, "Tulsa World" reported that many photographers stood atop "The Shakarian Hall" and recorded the ceremony through telephoto lenses. My grandfather was seated in the front row, as twenty-thousand guests heard Billy Graham deliver the dedicatory address.

Many years later "The Shakarian Hall" would be renamed.

Oral Roberts credited my grandfather as the one to put the first shovel in the dirt when breaking ground for Oral Roberts University. Oral explained how it was just Oral, his wife, his son and four other men on the bare five-hundred acres. These were the seven Co-Founders of ORU.

CLIFTON'S CAFETERIA

A crisp Saturday morning in October 1951, Grandfather woke up with excitement because he was having the first meeting of his new organization. The meeting was to be held on the second floor of Clifton's Cafeteria, in downtown Los Angeles. Grandfather knew with having Oral Roberts as his guest speaker they were sure to have overflowing crowds.

Grandfather enthusiastically invited everyone he could think of and began to spread the word, as he had done with every other meeting. This included all his business associates, their wives, and friends. The excitement was building in my Bobby's heart.

He had held many meetings previously, but this one was different. This meeting was specifically aligned with the prophecies given to him over the years. My grandfather believed the Lord's direction for him was finally coming together and becoming clear!

The much-anticipated Saturday morning finally arrived, and all the details were set. Grandmother would play the piano as she had so faithfully done for many of the meetings Grandfather organized. Oral Roberts was ready and honored to be the first guest speaker. Well over 300 guests were expected to attend. My grandfather didn't mind paying for everyone's breakfast, as he knew many would hear about God's love for the first time.

The air was chilly as my grandparents, and Oral Roberts drove together to Clifton's Cafeteria that Saturday morning for the meeting. The traffic was unusually heavy, and there were problems finding parking near the building. Quickly walking toward the cafeteria, holding my grandmother close with his arm around her waist, he almost swept her off her feet. My grandfather was thanking God with every step, knowing his mission was being fulfilled.

Removing his famous cream-colored Stetson hat, he climbed the wide staircase hearing his cowboy boots at every step.

Removing his famous cream-colored Stetson hat, my Grandfather, my Grandmother, and Oral Roberts excitedly entered Clifton's Cafeteria. As they climbed the wide staircase to the third floor, hearing his cowboy boots at every step, Grandfather began to wonder how many would attend. This moment had been gloriously replayed in his mind for months!

He had done everything as before following the same protocol like his other meetings. He hoped like many times previously; there would be standing room only. When he turned the corner, taking a deep breath, he looked around the room. He was overwhelmed by what he saw. He felt as if everything suddenly went into slow motion as he started to count. One, two, three . . . there were 18 people not including my grandparents and Oral Roberts!

THE BREAKTHROUGH MOMENT

My grandmother did not give Grandfather time to react to the turnout. Instead, she quickly moved to the old piano in the corner of the room and began playing her heart out. Grandfather looked around the room to see who was there. He saw his most loyal friends. He knew these men must have heard from the Lord. Due to their busy schedules, they still made time to come.

"This group of businessmen will grow and expand to a thousand chapters." As my grandmother sang the last hymn, Grandfather stood up to share his vision saying, "We are a group of ordinary businessmen. We are not going to hold meetings in a church but in comfortable and familiar settings. We are businessmen who care about other businessmen, and who have stories and testimonies of what God has done and is continuing to do in our lives." He went on to explain his vision. "In coming here today, we want to establish new avenues for people to share about the Lord."

As my grandfather heard himself talk, he tried his best to explain what he had in his heart concerning his vision. The eighteen in attendance did not appear to be inspired. They were fidgeting, but because of the small group size, no one could slip out unnoticed. So after saying just a few words, Grandfather turned the meeting over to Oral Roberts.

A THOUSAND CHAPTERS

To my grandfather's surprise, Oral began by sharing his appreciation for the small turnout. "Thank you God, for this small group which showed up," Oral Roberts continued by leading the group in prayer. "Lord, from the very beginning, this organization will be put together by You, and we give You all the honor which will come forth, as it is Your organization. The growth will be Your doing, with no man taking the glory."

After sharing a short but powerful message, Oral Roberts asked the eighteen people in front of him to stand. He began to pray boldly. "Lord, this organization will grow in Your might and power. Send it forth in Your strength around the world. Thank you Lord Jesus, for what You are going to do with this group which started here in downtown Los Angeles. This group of businessmen will grow and expand – to a thousand chapters!"

As Oral Roberts spoke the words, *a thousand chapters*, the handful of restless men and women came alive. They too suddenly saw the vision. Soon the little group, which had previously been looking at their watches, began to sing enthusiastically. As they sang the familiar lyrics, they took hold of each other's hands while marching in place. Each verse sounded louder than the previous until a fire was ignited in everyone's hearts!

Onward, Christian soldiers!
Marching as to war,
With the cross of Jesus
Going on before.

This was Grandfather's breakthrough moment. Their hearts being filled with faith, knowing what God was going to do. Everyone left Clifton's Cafeteria infused with excitement, but no one more so than my Bobby.

"Embedded in the unprecedented growth of Christendom in the past 100 years, the following statement embodies a significant pillar in supporting the aforementioned truth. The ministry Demos Shakarian founded, changed the world for the glory of Christ.

His ministry served as the catalytic platform, whereby countless marketplace leaders and entrepreneurs were experiencing the grace-filled message of Jesus. Without it, the world would not be the same!"

— **Samuel Rodriguez** • Pastor, New Season Christian Worship / National Hispanic Christian Leadership Conference

Memory Lane

Demos Shakarian

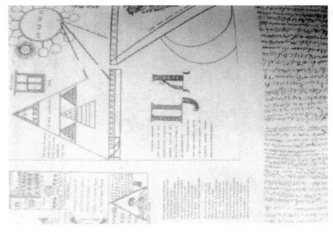

The Prophecy
and drawing of
the 11-year-old
"Boy Prophet."

Isaac standing
in the back row
surrounded
by his sisters.
His father and
mother are
seated. Little
sister Hamas
is sitting in the
middle.

919 Boston Street.

The first home
in Los Angeles,
California where my
family lived with
two other families,
upon arriving from
Armenia.

My grandmother Rose with little Steve next to her.
Aunt Geri in the middle and my dad Richard on the right.

My grandfather Demos

My grandmother Rose

Great-grandfather Isaac and Grandfather Demos.

Of course, with their Stetson Hats!

Three Generations working together!

My dad Richard, great-grandfather Isaac, and grandfather Demos.

Grandfather looking over one of his properties.

The Norwalk Shopping Center.

A farmer at heart, in his Reliance Dairy truck!

Reliance Dairy's
farm in
Bakersfield,
California.

Cows, Cows, and
more Cows!

Reliance Dairy

One of the first
drive-thru stores.

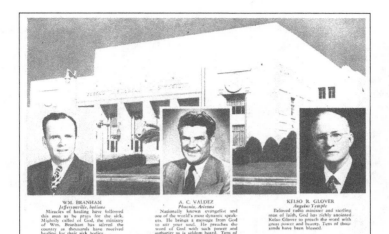

A newspaper advertisement Grandfather placed for meetings in Fresno, California.

My father Richard, grandfather Demos and great-grandfather Isaac.

Clifton's Cafeteria
Around the time Grandfather's organization held their first meeting!

The banner my grandfather displayed in his meetings.

President Ronald Reagan
and Demos Shakarian.

President Richard Nixon
and Demos Shakarian.

Rev. Billy Graham and my grandfather.

Grandfather always chose the best venues!

The Airlifts where hundreds of members in
my grandfather's organization traveled world-wide!

My grandparents at the airport ready to travel the world!

Conrad Hilton Hotel
Many of my grandfather's conventions were held there.
In the hope of getting a seat, the lines were endless!

Thousands gathered at my grandfather's meetings!

Demos Shakarian and Dr. Oral Roberts.

Kenneth and Gloria Copeland
with my grandparents, Demos and Rose Shakarian.

Great-grandfather Isaac holding me, his little Cynthia Rene'e!

With my grandfather . . . holding onto his every word!

Grandfather's Headquarters
on Figueroa Street in Los Angeles, California.

Grandfather on the
building site of the new
Headquarters for
his organization.

3150 Bear Street, Costa Mesa, California.
The International Headquarters is a landmark in the community.

The Christmas Cheer celebration.
Grandfather's last Christmas.

Christmas,
the Armenian Way!

With my
precious dad,
Richard Shakarian.

My beautiful
mother,
Evangeline.
(Vangie)

That's me on a Reliance Dairy pony!

My grandparents, Momie and Bobby.

A note from my grandparents in 1975!

Xmas - 1995

Dear Cynthia Reneé,

      This is our heritage which God has given us and which we are passing on to you.

      We love you and pray God's blessing on your life all the days of your life.

        Your Momie + Bobby.

Rose. Prov. 3: 5-6

       Phil - 4: 13

Demos

Deut. 28 1-14

From my
grandfather's
humble
beginnings, he
would end up
inspiring
millions with
God's love.

One of the greatest joys
of his life was loving,
encouraging, and praying for others.
It was his purpose in life!

My beginnings
in Real Estate.

Continuing Grandfather's legacy by serving others at
Christmas Cheer, with my dad and my grandfather.

At the podium sharing at an
FGBMFI International Convention
and many places around the world!

Dear Bobby and Momie,

I dedicate this book to you both.

Every moment we have shared together, I cherish.
Your lives have given me the way to live,
the way to love, and the way to be.

You have encouraged me to never accept the less
but always expect the more!

With Love,
Cynthia Renée

CHAPTER TWELVE

The Twelve-Month Journey of Faith

❧

For the next year, my grandfather held breakfast meetings at Clifton's Cafeteria every Saturday morning. He would invite many wonderful guest speakers. The people who attended would eat breakfast on the main floor and then climb the stairs to the second-floor banquet room for the meeting.

The entire first year was met with no growth at all. Making matters worse, some pastors were concerned this group may affect their church attendance and offerings. They didn't understand this new concept. Grandfather's organization wasn't a church but a business men's fellowship. He was a huge support to churches in the area and encouraged everyone to attend their local church, and get involved. Unfortunately, the opposition was still at hand.

HIS JOURNEY BEGINS

The weeks turned into months, and my grandfather started to grow increasingly discouraged. He believed when God is part of something; He blesses it. In the natural, things were not looking good at all. It did not appear the Saturday

What will it take for the vision God has for me to become a reality?

morning meetings at Clifton's Cafeteria were being blessed.

Grandfather was working at the dairy every day and his nights were spent promoting the meetings. By summer he had grown weary from the long days and nights. Also for the continuing small attendance at the Saturday breakfast meetings. He felt people were inspired hearing how the Lord was helping others at their workplace, yet attendance was minimal.

As always Grandfather put all of his energy, expertise and his funds into advertising the meetings. As he had previously done, he sent out fliers, advertised on the radio, and continued using the same model he had so successfully applied in the past, but nothing seemed to work. Grandfather wondered, *what will it take for the vision God has for me to become a reality?*

My Bobby was determined to fulfill his purpose while on this earth. He knew he heard from God but had never encountered problems getting attendance like he was now. So he did everything he could think of. After all, he was already offering a free breakfast. He bought more radio time and was broadcasting part of the meeting. He traveled up and down the California coast telling everyone he knew about the meetings. Finally, he even ventured to other states, broadcasting the meetings as far as the East Coast which was thousands of miles away. He was describing to everyone along the way about his vision, but nothing was working!

He was a huge support to churches in the area.

Week upon week, the same familiar faces attended the meetings at Clifton's Cafeteria. Not only was there a low turnout, but

Grandfather was funding all the expenses of the meetings. At this point, even my grandmother was disillusioned. She could not understand the lack of progress and voiced her concerns to Grandfather saying, "You must have missed God!" She wasn't sure they should continue, especially because everything my grandfather touched previously had been a great success.

A PROPHECY BY SMITH WIGGLESWORTH

Around this time he invited David du Plessis to speak, fondly referred to as "Mr. Pentecost." As his nickname suggests, David was extremely active in the *World Pentecostal Conference.* After the meeting, David approached my grandfather to share his thoughts. "What a wonderful organization this is!" David du Plessis told Grandfather, "Just imagine a worldwide fellowship of ordinary businessmen, sharing the love of God all over the world!"

David's inspiring words were encouraging to Grandfather, but he did not know how God's vision in him would play out. David du Plessis seemed to be drawn to my grandfather's vision. He told Grandfather this had to be a Divinely inspired idea. He said this would be the next great move of God!

Wanting to encourage Grandfather, David du Plessis shared a prophecy given by Smith Wigglesworth, who was well known as a man who hears from God and was able to recognize God's seasons and times.

Describing the prophecy in detail, he quoted Wigglesworth's words, "First there would be a move among the layman, next other religions would be affected by the power of God, and finally whole Nations will come to the Lord. Countries which people thought would never turn to Christ, will indeed make Him their Lord and Savior."

GOING TO LONDON

David du Plessis invited my grandparents to join him in London where he said, Grandfather could share his vision at a meeting he was having there. My grandparents decided to go thinking; *maybe this will be the jumpstart needed.* With their family members unsure of their safety flying so far away, they promised to take separate flights to London. They were reminded, "You have three children to consider."

As they were leaving for the airport my grandparent's extended family said goodbye; like it was the last time they would ever see them again. Words of advice were given, and tears were shed. It was a very dramatic scene.

The trip went speeding downhill from there!!!

They had an overnight stop in New York, taking separate flights again until finally arriving in London. Sadly, David du Plessis greeted them with some disappointing news. To his surprise, the people were questioning how a dairyman could be the head of such an organization because they expected, an ordained minister to be in charge.

My grandparents and David du Plessis were determined not to give up. They went around to other meetings and conferences sharing about this wonderful new organization, but could not get one person interested in becoming a leader in their city and start a new chapter.

Realizing they no longer had a reason to continue their stay in London, they flew separately to Germany. They were going to meet a friend of Grandfather's, who was a pastor of a church which had been affected by the bombing in Hamburg, Germany.

Trying to help his friend, my grandfather had shipped a huge Tent to Germany to hold meetings in, because his friends' church had been demolished in the bombing.

> *Grandfather had shipped a huge Tent to Germany so meetings could be held.*

The pastor wanted to show my grandparents the area which was bombed, but more importantly, he wanted to show them something else. He wanted my grandparents to see because of the Tent Grandfather sent to them; they were able to still have church. The members of the congregation could not wait to express their appreciation to Grandfather for his generosity.

A MIRACLE IN GERMANY

Arriving in Hamburg in July 1952, my grandparents were surprised to see everything was still in ruins. The pastor shared their miracle story of events the day of the bombing. They were inside their church when the air-raid sirens blared. Everyone ran to the underground shelter, where 300 people crowded to safety. Suddenly they heard bombs going off above them. When they felt it was safe to come out, the doors seemed to be welded together from the heat of the explosions. They were trapped! Breathing became difficult in such a confined space.

The pastor turned to God in prayer, "Lord we are in need of a miracle as our doors are melted shut! Help us; we don't know how long we will be able to stay in here." Suddenly, a bomb hit nearby and the force of the explosion burst the shelter's doors wide open. As everyone hurriedly ran out of the open doors, they were screaming from the top of their lungs, "Thank you, Jesus!" In astonishment, they looked at what was left of their church where they had been sitting only moments before. Everything in sight was in ruins, yet they were all alive. Halleluiah!

After spending time with the congregation, Grandfather prayed a prayer of thanksgiving to the Lord, for answering their prayer and keeping everyone safe. He also thanked the Lord for allowing him to be used in sending the huge Tent to the pastor. He was honored to be linked spiritually with this faithful congregation. They then shared a beautiful meal together, prepared by the Congregation in honor of my grandparents.

VENICE, ITALY

Before heading back to California, Grandmother wanted to make a quick trip to Venice. She thought this would be her last time she would travel so far away from home. Little did my grandparents know, soon they would be circling the globe sharing the love of Jesus with the world!

Grandmother was looking forward to their romantic gondola ride down the Venetian canals.

Excited to be in Venice, Grandmother was looking forward to their romantic gondola ride down the Venetian canals. She envisioned going through the luxurious waterways of Italy. Unfortunately, that's not what happened.

My grandfather was taking pictures from the train window enjoying the scenery. As he leaned out the window to get a better view, he felt something sharp enter his eye. It turned out to be a sharp stone, and it was in too deep for Grandmother to pull out.

The pain was excruciating. They raced to the hotel, and when the manager saw the condition Grandfather was in, he immediately called the doctor. This was an emergency!

As the doctor flashed a light in my grandfather's eye, he thought he might pass out from the pain. Grandfather said it was the most excruciating pain he had ever felt in his life. The doctor explained this was very serious and he would need to go to the hospital and have it removed.

Grandmother calmly suggested that before going to the hospital, they should pray and get God involved. Grandfather had been in so much pain; he couldn't believe he had not yet prayed for God's help. They immediately came together in agreement, as Grandmother began to thank the Lord for removing the stone from Grandfather's eye and keeping his eyesight safe. She was praying in pure faith, not looking at the current situation but believing God was going to protect his eye.

As she was praying, Grandfather said he no longer felt pain. He asked her if she saw anything in his eye. Next, he asked the doctor to check his eye again. The doctor looked sternly at them, making sure they understood the urgency of the situation. "You need to hurry and get this man to the hospital!" he exclaimed. Thinking maybe because my grandparents were Americans, they did not understand the necessity of going to the hospital immediately.

To appease them, he flashed his light once again in Grandfathers' eye before exclaiming, "It's not there! I don't see anything in your eye! There is not even a sign of injury!" God had completely healed Grandfather's eye. My grandparents began thanking and praising the Lord for this miracle. They looked into each other's eyes as they both couldn't get the words out fast enough, "Let's go home!"

THE WELCOMING COMMITTEE

Arriving back home at the Los Angeles airport, my grandfather was ready to kiss the ground as he got off the plane. It had been quite a trip! Of course, keeping their promise, again they flew on separate planes. When both their planes had finally landed, all they wanted to do was to hug their three kids. Grandfather, knowing he went through a horrendous experience, also saw how God had used him.

I can imagine their arrival back in California went something like this. The welcoming committee at the airport was in full force, as members from both sides of the family were all there to greet them. As Steve ran into my grandmothers' arms, my grandfather embraced my dad Richard and my Aunt Geri. As excited as their children were to see them, they couldn't wait to see the souvenir's their parents had brought back for them.

> *Grandfather knowing he went through a horrendous experience also saw how God had used him.*

My grandparents still beaming over being united with their children, headed to my Great-Bobby Isaac's house for a big celebratory feast. I know what you're thinking. A feast, again! Shish kabob, rice pilaf, shaka loof . . ! That would be a definite "Yes!"

As usual all occasions, whether happy or sad, revolve around the dinner table, as everyone came together to enjoy conversation and good food. This could be a clue as to why some Armenians' are not known for their slim waistlines! The entire family breathed a collective sigh of relief. My grandparents were home!

"As a young, Baptist businessman in the mid-1960's I was invited to a meeting in Cleveland, Tennessee. I was told the founder of this organization was a very successful businessman, and since I was a businessman myself, I agreed to go.

I walked into that meeting, and I reached out to shake the hand of the first man I was introduced to but instead, the man pulled me in and hugged me. I had never had anyone do that before. At first, everything in me wanted to get out of there but out of respect for the man that brought me, I decided to stay.

The meeting began, and everyone started singing with such joy. I had never heard anything like that in my life. I left the meeting thinking it would be my last time attending, but then the strangest thing happened. I would be driving down the road or lying down at night to sleep, and I would hear them singing over again in my head. I had this feeling in my heart; there was something to those people. So by the time the next meeting came, I couldn't wait to go.

Several months later, my life changed forever when I had the opportunity to meet Demos Shakarian! I don't know of another person who has had any greater impact on the full gospel world than that of Demos. It was through Demos I was introduced to the moving of the Spirit, I received my prayer language and learned how to lay hands on the sick. He was a tremendous man of faith, and I had the honor of ministering in healing meetings with him on numerous occasions and witnessed hundreds of miracles.

Demos was more than a good friend to me, I considered him one of my closest friends.

The Lord used Demos Shakarian and his vision to launch me into the purpose and plan of God for my life. I am truly thankful I didn't run out of the building all those years ago!"

— Norvel Hayes • Norvel Hayes Ministries

CHAPTER THIRTEEN

The Vision that Changed Everything!

One summer afternoon not long after turning 17 years old, it was exciting to be cruising in my first car. I was a new graduate of High School and driving my maroon Camaro, with not a care in the world. As I headed towards my grandparent's home, I felt free and believed I could do anything!

That was the time I started my training in Real Estate believing I would become an expert in Real Estate, just like my grandfather. I was a young girl with big plans. I arrived at my grandparent's home and knocked on the door. My grandmother invited me in leading me to one of my favorite rooms in their home, her breakfast room. It always felt so cheerful and cozy. On one side of the room stood a built-in hutch with glass doors and crystal knobs, which was the home of my grandmother's *Royal Albert Old Country Rose Collection China.*

As Grandmother poured our coffee, I thought about all my family ancestors, who drank from the same china cups, and all the fascinating people who dined at my grandparent's home, eating from this very same china. I particularly cared for this room because it was cheerful and bright due to the large rectangular windows surrounding the room.

My distant thoughts were interrupted as my grandmother Momie asked; "Cynthia jan, would you like more coffee?" I especially loved when she would sometimes call me *Cynthia jan*. An endearing term, it would be like saying: "Cynthia darling or dear."

It was in their breakfast room I spent so many afternoons deep in conversation with my grandmother. I cherished every moment and today was no exception. Momie found joy in seeing me interested in her and her life. I soaked up every word. I loved hearing how the Lord usually confirmed His direction to both of my grandparents. What a blessing it was listening to the dialogue between them straight from my grandmother. Hearing her tell about their heart-to-heart talks brought me closer to both of my grandparents.

THE LAST MEETING?

In December 1952, an evangelist friend, Tommy Hicks came to stay with my grandparents for the week. It was a welcome visit even though my grandfather was feeling pretty low. He felt that his vision for his organization had come to a plateau. Tommy arrived on a Friday evening, settled in and sat down to eat the delicious meal my grandmother prepared in his honor. Over dinner, my grandfather discussed with him about the Saturday morning meetings, which had been taking place for

Attendance has not grown by a single person.

a year now. "It's disheartening," he confided. "Attendance has not grown by a single person. In fact, there are often fewer people than when we originally started."

Then he spoke words which were hard to say, "I am not sure God has blessed this, and I do not understand why. I know the idea was His idea, yet He has not touched the heart of the people who've attended. No one has started a second chapter. In fact, sometimes I think they are coming to the meetings only as a favor to me."

My grandfather had a heavy heart and tears welled in his eyes. Then he made a confession. "We have been meeting every Saturday morning for a year, and it's clear there is no real interest. I have decided that tomorrow will be the last meeting. I will let the members know we can work together again next summer to sponsor Tent meetings in Los Angeles."

The atmosphere was so thick with the presence of the Holy Spirit it was tangible.

Tommy could feel the unrest in my grandfather's heart, and he wanted to continue listening and helping my grandfather work through this difficult time. The two friends stayed at the dining room table until almost midnight discussing the matter.

Grandfather shared some of the highlights of the meetings, including the bright light which would shine on the faces of those who had something to contribute. "I have never left a Saturday morning meeting at Clifton's Cafeteria, where I didn't learn how to love God more or love people more," he humbly told Tommy.

Moments later Tommy Hicks stood to retire. He offered to help my grandmother clear the dining room table. My grandfather announced, I am going to the living room to pray, and I'm not leaving until I hear from God. Tommy made his way to the bedroom Grandmother had prepared for him. He was staying in my father, Richard's room who was away.

As my grandfather entered the living room, the same overwhelming presence of the Holy Spirit which had descended upon him when he was thirteen-years-old, filled the room.

"No, I will never doubt You, Lord! I will never doubt Your power!"

The atmosphere was so thick with the presence of the Holy Spirit, it *was tangible*. He fell to his knees in prayer knowing God was there with him.

THE VISION!

My grandmother softly walked into the room, sat at the organ and played songs worshipping God. As the music filled the room, Grandfather began to praise the Lord. He felt the *invisible warm blanket* wrap around him once again, as he continued in prayer. As the power of the Holy Spirit fell upon him, time stood still, and the room permeated with an overwhelming love for the Lord.

Suddenly my grandfather heard the familiar words he had heard before, "Demos, do you doubt My power?" With Grandfather kneeling on the rug as he prayed, he realized he had depended upon his own abilities to bring growth. He realized he was trying to increase attendance by his own strength. He was working as though it was up to him to raise the organization himself.

This is not what Oral Roberts had prayed during the first meeting. When Oral prayed, "Let the growth of this Fellowship grow in Your strength and power alone." At that moment, my grandfather cried out for forgiveness from the Lord, for trying to put all the pieces together himself. "No, I will never doubt

You, Lord! I will never doubt Your power!" he exclaimed.

As he prayed, my grandmother continued playing the organ and as she worshiped, the presence of God grew stronger. Then she began to pray in the Holy Spirit when suddenly she stopped and started prophesying. The Lord speaking through her said,

> "My son, I knew you before you were born and I have directed your steps. Now I am going to show you your purpose in life. It was for this reason you were born. Look not to the right or to the left, but continue therein. Fear not! Fear not, I am leading you. You are in the center of my will. I am with you!"

And with that, the Lord began to show Grandfather a vision of what God would do through this group.

AROUND THE WORLD ... TWICE!

Suddenly, my grandfather felt as though he had left his living room. The heavens had opened, and he was lifted into the sky, looking down at the city of Downey. His viewpoint

They looked like "dead men standing!"

broadened as he continued to rise. He could see the entire United States and then the whole earth. Now above the clouds, he saw the world turn slowly below him seeing every continent. His perspective began to change, as he traveled around the world ... twice!

The first time he saw millions of people standing side by side. He saw men from every nation throughout the world. Zooming in on a few of them, he could see every detail on their faces. He noticed their different style of dress and their varying skin colors. Though he was amazed at this unfamiliar experience, he was overwhelmed with concern for the men he saw. They appeared to have no light inside of them. He described them as "dead men standing."

My grandfather, extremely upset by what he was seeing and the look of suffering on their faces, cried out to the Lord, "Why are all these people suffering? They seem so lonely! Who are these people standing side by side? No life appears to be in them. They look as though they are made of stone, and they have no connection with each other. Lord, please help them, they are hurting!"

Again through Grandmother, the Lord spoke though she had no idea what Grandfather was witnessing.

"My son, what you will see now is about to happen. Look not to the right or the left. You are in the center of my will. It will come to pass. I am leading you. You are ... in the center of my will!"

With that, the scenery changed as he saw men from around the world a second time. All the people of different nationalities and colors looked up, smiling and full of joy with the glow of God on their faces. Their hands were lifted towards Heaven, praising and worshipping the Lord together. They now seemed to be connected, as if they were a support and encouragement to each other. Many were standing with their arms linked to the man next to him. Everything around the people which had kept them isolated was now gone. With their newfound support from one another, everyone was full

To destroy loneliness and isolation and share the love of God with everyone around the world!

of life and showed the love of God on their faces; as well as love to each other!

LIQUID FIRE!

Now beaming with a smile which grew from ear to ear, Grandfather looked around to find himself back in his living room lying face down. When my grandfather arose from the living room floor, he was trembling from the power of God. My grandmother excitedly asked, "What just happened? Did the Lord show you something . . . anything?" She knew the Lord must have taken over. Grandfather rushed to explain. He was so excited that he couldn't get the words out fast enough, telling Grandmother what the Lord had shown him.

He told her in detail everything he saw and all the things they would accomplish. Using God's power, timing, and strength, they would reach across the nations and around the

> *It was like liquid fire coming down!*

world. Of course, this would all be God's work. No man could accomplish this using his own methods.

My Bobby described how the Lord showed him his purpose, which was to bring all faiths, nationalities, and races together. To destroy loneliness and isolation, and share the love of God with everyone around the world!

By now it was past 3:00 a.m. My grandparents were excited and couldn't think about going to sleep. They couldn't wait to tell their friend Tommy about the incredible vision, and what God was going to do. They walked towards the room he was sleeping in and saw the light shining beneath the door. Grandfather knocked on Tommy's bedroom door, and Tommy answered immediately. My grandfather was surprised to see him standing there still dressed in the suit he had worn at dinner, which by now was a wrinkled mess.

Tommy began to explain, "As I knelt down to pray, the power of the Holy Spirit filled the bedroom in such a powerful way I could not stand up. In fact, the Spirit fell so unbelievably strong over the entire house. It was a power like I had never felt before. It was like liquid fire coming down! I just continued praying, lying on the floor." "Demos!" said my grandmother. "This is confirmation of what the Lord just showed you. "Yes!" Grandfather exclaimed. "The meetings are going to continue. This is not the end. This is just the beginning of what God will do!"

"I want to say a few words about a man I believe God called to touch the lives of untold millions all over the world. A man who not only understood business but also knew how to reach out to those both inside and outside the church — and that man was Demos Shakarian.

What an honor and a blessing it is that I had the privilege of knowing this visionary and being a part of Demos' organization.

When I went into full-time ministry in 1978, because of this association, it began to open doors of opportunity which I never thought would be opened to me. This was all due in part to Demos Shakarian and his obedience to the vision God birthed in his heart. I can't thank God enough for this wonderful man, for the measure of faith he left for all of us, and for his work which continues.

I'm so excited his granddaughter Cynthia Shakarian, has written this book about his life and legacy. I believe you will be blessed by it and it will minister to you greatly.

Thank you, Demos! Every time I go to a meeting and preach the Gospel, I remember my beginnings started with your ministry."

—Jesse Duplantis • Jesse Duplantis Ministries

CHAPTER FOURTEEN

Covering the Globe

"*H* is whole life he worked on the dairy farm
building *Reliance Dairy*.
It was Demos Shakarian's passion.
But spreading God's love, was his heart!
His greatest desire was to
follow his dream and fulfill his purpose!"
— **Cynthia Shakarian**

The next day was cold, a wintery Saturday morning in December 1952. My grandparents arrived at Clifton's Cafeteria.

Two men had already arrived for the morning meeting, one of whom was a member of the board. Grandfather was surprised to see his friend, Miner Arganbright, there. Just last week this same man had told my grandfather *the whole organization wasn't worth a nickel*. Yet there he was, waiting for the meeting to begin. As Grandfather approached his friend, Miner reached into his pocket and said, "Demos, I have something for you."

Grandfather was confused. What could this man who was so discouraged with the progress of the meetings have to offer him? Maybe it's his resignation from the *Board of Directors*? To Grandfather's surprise, Miner Arganbright handed him a check made out to his organization in the amount for $1,000!

THE BIRTH OF THE MAGAZINE

Up until this point, no one had donated to the organization. As Grandfather accepted the check, he said, "Last week you told me the whole organization wasn't worth a nickel. What happened?" "That was last week," his friend replied.

He thought;
Wow, that was
fast Lord!

"Early this morning as I awoke, I heard God say, 'Demos' vision is about to go around the world, and I want you to make the first donation!' So there it is, Demos. There is your first donation. And this is just the beginning of my donations to help spread the love of God."

Grandfather could hardly believe it! He thought; *Wow that was fast Lord!* Before he had a chance to respond, another man approached him. "Hello Demos, my name is Thomas Nickel," said the man. "God also spoke to me last night. I heard him say I needed to be at this Saturday morning meeting. I live several hundred miles away, so I had to leave during the night to make it. I came here to offer you my printing press."

"Your printing press?" my grandfather asked, confused and unsure of what he would do with a printing press. "Yes," confirmed Mr. Nickel. "It is so you can put out a magazine. I kept hearing your organization is going to go around the world, but it needed a voice to get started." Grandmother, who was standing nearby looked at Grandfather. As they had done so many times before, they thought of the name together. "The Business Men's Voice," they said at once, naming the magazine right then and there.

My grandfather went on to say, "A magazine could feature many of the miracles God was performing in the member's

lives. We could highlight one person's story on the front of every
magazine, and include other stories
inside with announcements of our
upcoming meetings." And just that
quickly the official magazine was born.

> *To inspire and encourage
> one another with
> all the gifts of the
> Holy Spirit flowing.*

In the years that would follow my grandfather looked back on the meeting that day with such joy. He knew both Miner Arganbright and Thomas Nickel were agents of the Lord. Whereas the day before he thought he might be holding the very last meeting. In fact, the meeting turned out to be just the beginning. As Grandfather described it there was a new joy, an excitement about what the Lord was doing, and going to do, through this new organization.

My grandparents drove home that day blessed and in awe of how the Lord turned things around so quickly. Little did they know what would happen around the world and how many millions of lives would be changed. I'm sure; they never imagined just how far and wide my Bobby's vision was going to reach!

It wasn't long before Clifton's Cafeteria was packed every Saturday morning, with up to 700 people overflowing down the grand staircase. People from all over Southern California would attend the crowded, standing-room-only meeting. Due to the crowds, the fire marshal would also become one of his regular visitors!

EXPLODING WORLDWIDE

The goal of sharing Christ in an organization of businessmen was realized. Grandfather encouraged some of the members to start chapters in their cities. "This is how we can reach more people," he explained.

Soon, other chapters were established. Just a short time later my grandparents began to travel all over the world. As Grandfather had envisioned, people were coming together to inspire and encourage one another, with all the gifts of the Holy Spirit flowing.

Grandfather displayed love to all. He would wrap his caring arms around the homeless and invite them to the meetings as well. Regardless whether they were living on the street or a top businessman, he would give equal attention to both.

Over time the chapters continued growing and multiplying. The original group which began at Clifton's Cafeteria eventually grew into ten groups. Forty-two chapters had sprouted just in the Los Angeles area. It was an explosive growth. Soon chapters were found all over the United States. Then all over the world!

Grandfather's organization was not having just another meeting. It became a destination families planned vacations around! The meetings were inviting. They warmly welcomed everyone regardless of race, religious affiliation, or economic status. It was the place to experience the fullness of the Holy Spirit, and hear the inspirational stories of how God was changing lives.

Now calls were coming in continually from around the world with requests for Grandfather to come to their city. His organization was experiencing a supernatural increase!

VICE-PRESIDENT RICHARD M. NIXON

In 1954 my grandfather held a convention for five days in our nation's capital, Washington D.C. It was at the beautiful

Omni Shoreham Hotel, the site of many significant moments including inaugural balls. One of the speakers was Richard M. Nixon, who at the time was the current Vice-President of the United States. He was the keynote speaker at the men's breakfast meeting. Members of Congress, local residents, and others from all over the country attended.

Grandfather gave love and attention to everyone!

The inspiring evening meetings held in the Constitution Hall, included powerful messages from speakers William Branham, Jack Coe, and A.C. Valdez, Jr. The services were also filled with great testimonies from many men, which blessed all who were in attendance.

Ending this historic event, Oral Roberts spoke. His message on "The Burning Bush" was a revelatory experience moving seven-hundred people, with many dedicating their lives to the Lord.

HELPING TO CHANGE
A CITY, A COUNTRY, A NATION . . . THE WORLD!

During the '50s and '60s, racial segregation was an issue in many parts of the nation. My grandfather was preparing for his World Convention to be held in Atlanta, Georgia.

Over one-thousand rooms had been reserved for five nights, in preparation for the large numbers

Grandfather moved to ensure everyone would be welcomed.

of people who were expected to attend. Grandfather had purchased radio time to promote the convention, booked the speakers, ordered advertising and printed registration forms.

Grandfather would not allow any man, woman or child to be discriminated.

Everything was in place for a standing room only convention.

It was sure to be extremely well-attended. As usual, the attendees were expected to be of different religions and ethnicities. Then the hotel management heard that African-Americans' would be attending as well. When the hotel discovered the anticipated racial composition, management offered to make identical accommodations for the African-Americans' at a nearby hotel, using closed-circuit TV transmission to broadcast the convention.

My Bobby was saddened when he heard of the Hotel's discrimination. Jesus so loved the world as my grandfather loved all. He did what he felt was the right thing to do. Though only a month away, the convention in Atlanta was CANCELED!

He would not allow any man, woman or child to be discriminated. He decided to move the entire convention over 1,400 miles away to Denver, Colorado. Where everyone would be welcomed and accommodated *equally*. Even though he would be losing time and money, his decision was made. "We're moving!" Grandfather exclaimed without giving it a second thought.

Upon hearing what happened in Atlanta, I continue to be as proud of Grandfather now as when I first heard this story. He never ceased to amaze me at how he was a man with wisdom and discernment beyond his years. A man who helped to change a city, a country, a nation, the world!

True to form, he treated everyone the same. My Bobby had the gift to unite people from different communities, bringing them together to break down the barriers of race and denominations.

"The Shakarian Legacy heralds the life of a pioneer which blazed a trail that has impacted literally millions around the world. I will never forget my first invitation to go and minister in song at one of Demos' meetings. It was a pivotal point in my life.

Seeing people from all backgrounds and denominations worshipping in the same room was overwhelming for me as a teenager, living in a very racially divided community.

What Demos Shakarian did is what happened in the book of Acts when the church was birthed. This man of God helped to birth a revolution of change in Christendom, which we are still feeling today.

I believe this book from his granddaughter, Cynthia Shakarian, will give you a bird's eye view of what God did, and how He did it through this man who was willing to say, 'Yes.' You will be enlightened and stirred!

May God raise up many more men and women who will hearken to this generation's clarion call, to help change this divided culture, into a God-breathed culture!"

— **Judy Jacobs** • Co-Pastor / Dwelling Place Church International

REV. BILLY GRAHAM

On July 6, 1962, Billy Graham spoke at Grandfather's 10th Annual Convention, at the Olympic Hotel in Seattle, Washington. Receiving a tremendous welcome, he shared with the excited crowd a compelling message; "Something is Happening ... a move of the Spirit of God!" He went on to tell the members of Grandfather's organization, "I thank God for you, and your steadfastness in the faith!"

The new Reliance Dairy's drive-through store.

Many others also shared how the power of God had changed their life, including; my Great-Bobby, Isaac, who delivered a powerful testimony. As John Osteen was praying for those who wanted to receive the Holy Spirit, the power of God filled the Grand Ballroom. Lester Sumrall then prayed for those in need of God's healing power.

The Youth Banquet was receiving the same anointing. Four-hundred-eighty teenagers heard a life-changing message from Dr. Oral Roberts, who shared with them to "expect great things from God!" My dad, Richard, who lead the group also gave a faith-filled inspiring message. Now that's a convention!

EXPANDING THE FAMILY BUSINESS

In 1953 my grandfather had a new innovative idea for marketing the milk from Reliance Dairy. This was the beginning of a drive-through milk service. He believed he could sell the milk for less money compared to the milk bought in a store. It didn't take long for my grandfather to put all the pieces in place and turn his new idea into an up-and-running, drive-through dairy.

No seat belts!
No sunscreen!
How did we do it?

Knowing how to take advantage of marketing concepts, he held a huge "Grand Opening" at the new Reliance Dairy's drive-through store. With banners, mailers, radio announcements, and newspaper ads, it was guaranteed to be a hit. He brought in entertainment, including pony rides for the kids and a singer to entertain the adults. City and state officials even attended the ribbon-cutting ceremony!

This drive-through prototype caught on quickly. My Bobby and his father, Isaac soon duplicated the drive-through dairy many times over.

They offered their customers milk, eggs, cottage cheese, buttermilk, bacon and fruit punch when opening its first location in Downey. It was the first modern-day fast food model for dairy products. People would drive in, place their order and in minutes would be handed their groceries.

A customer remembered it like this:

"In our gas guzzling, seatbelt-less red Plymouth Suburban wagon full of non-sunscreen wearing kids, my mother would stop at the drive–thru *Reliance Dairy* on Beach Blvd, to buy half gallon glass containers of milk and bright red fruit punch!"

Isn't it amazing how we all managed to survive through this era? No seat belts! No sunscreen! How did we do it?

THREE GENERATIONS

By this time, my father Richard was working in the family business and was in charge of running and operating all the Drive-in stores. His business skills contributed significantly to the success of this new venture, and the growth multiplied substantially under his leadership.

This was a dream come true for my Great-Bobby, as now three generations were working together!

He looked outside the box and un-wrapped the gifts God had for him!!

Isaac and Demos also secured the right to sell their dairy products at various retail outlets, including grocery store chains. This brought in even more profits. By 1965, the drive-thru dairies totaled more than a dozen and would become the most well-known of the Shakarian ventures.

"In 1963 early into my pastorate at Anaheim Christian Center, later evolving into Melodyland Christian Center, our congregation became very involved in Demos' Conventions. I will never forget the day I was able to see the authentic 'dairy farmer' in Demos Shakarian.

One sweltering summer day my wife, Allene and I headed north up Highway 99 to California's central valley, to attend the grand opening of Demos' flagship dairy farm. Pulling into the crowded parking lot, we were joined by many others also invited for the ribbon-cutting ceremony.

Walking towards the entrance, we suddenly noticed our shoes started sticking to the pavement due to the tremendous heat. Once inside the luxurious air-conditioned barn, peering through a huge plate glass window, we were able to observe rows and rows of cows being milked by high tech machines. Although we had come to celebrate the opening of a dairy farm, instead we all had church. Demos led us in singing, testimonies, and praise; finishing with a prayer of dedication.

I realized that day, not only was this Armenian businessman a trailblazer in streamlining dairy farming production, he was also a shepherd in feeding and tending God's flock.

One of the conventions I remember most vividly was held in Phoenix, Arizona. What a magnetic meeting! There, I met many outstanding executives from the Orange County/ Los Angeles area, who were directly involved in Demos' ministry. Darrell Hon, a champion business owner, was one of those. Another notable professional was, Shannon Vandruff of Cinderella Homes, featured in Readers Digest for building the first upscale tract homes in Southern California.

'Demos Shakarian was also a man secure in his calling. He never tried to become someone else. It was evident that God had sent him to touch men in the marketplace and that was his only focus.

Demos appreciated the local church. He encouraged his partners to find a church and become involved. One of the things I respected most was his intensive drive towards soul winning. He realized the benefits of plugging into the Holy Spirit.

He also knew how to 'do it up right,' by hosting his international events at the most elegant hotels and boldest ballrooms. Successful business owners came from all over the world to be in some of those meetings.

I remember the crusade in New York City as being particularly outstanding. Kathryn Kuhlman was the featured speaker. The Holy Spirit's presence was ominous. In fact, some of the food workers busily preparing meals in the back of the hotel and listening to Miss Kuhlman's live service were not immune. Suddenly while scurrying around, setting tables and stirring pots of food, a heavy move of the Spirit invaded the kitchen area. Without any prompting, several of those dear food workers began to fall under the power, like dominos. There was such a move of the Holy Spirit in that meeting; it was infectious. That's because the Supernatural... is always so Natural!

Though I have many influences in my life to draw from, I will always honor Demos Shakarian as a lifelong friend, who had such an important impact on me as a young evangelist and pastor. He was a man who decided to look outside the box and unwrap the gifts and callings God had for him!"

— **Ralph Wilkerson** • Founder / Melodyland Christian Center

CHAPTER FIFTEEN

A Legacy of Love

My grandfather seemed to find special moments to reminisce with me. I can remember one of these moments when he sat down next to me and playfully commented on my burgundy corduroy-flare pants, crème embroidered peasant-top, and suede ankle boots.

I exclaimed, "Bobby, this is what all the girls are wearing right now!" Smiling with that familiar grin, he replied, "What happened to your business dress, heels, and pearls?" Knowing he was just teasing with me, I played along. "Bobby! I'm only 19-years-old, and I have to dress up like that for work every day. Selling Real Estate, I have to look much older than I am. Today, I'm comfortable and sitting next to you, ready to hear more about your life." Oh, how I loved sitting side by side with him!

As my Bobby reminisced about the incredible adventure his life had become, he expressed how happy he was that his father had been alive to see the growth of his organization. After all, he had played a tremendous role in helping my grandfather's vision become a reality. While talking, we were interrupted by a phone call. With Grandfather still speaking on the phone, my mind began to drift to the fond memories I had of my great-grandfather Isaac.

GREAT-BOBBY ISAAC

I remember Great-Bobby Isaac living on the same property as my grandparents. With the property being so large, there was a long winding cement path curving to connect the two homes. It was surrounded by large beautiful trees. As a little girl, it felt like I was following *The Yellow-Brick Road*! I loved going back and forth between my grandparent's one story home and my great-grandfather's large Spanish-style two-story home. Riding my 4-wheeled bike called a Surrey, between the two homes. It was a carriage with a bench seat for two in the front and one or two in the back, with a canopy top. As a child, I must have ridden that Surrey for miles!

The home Great-Bobby, Isaac had once shared with my great-grandmother had dark Spanish tile steps, which curved in an "L" shape. One of my favorite activities was to sit at the top of the stairs and bounce my way down, one step at a time until I hit the last stair. It was particularly fun because I loved watching the joy spread across my great-grandfather, Isaac's face as he watched me play on the stairs. Though Great-grandfather had broad shoulders from years of working on the farm, he was not a huge man, but he had a presence to me which was larger than life. How thankful I am to have these special memories with him.

My grandfather often told me he could never have accomplished all he did without the support of his father. Even as he was growing older, Isaac took care of the family dairy business, allowing my grandfather to put God's business first. This

> *Great-grandfather Isaac played a tremendous role in helping my grandfather's vision become a reality.*

gave Grandfather the freedom to travel and fulfill his vision, without feeling pressure to tend to Reliance Dairy's daily needs.

A PHILANTHROPIST

Great-grandfather Isaac was very civic minded, helping many in his city. He owned a multi-million-dollar development center, called *Norwalk Shopping Center* and many other real estate properties.

Isaac was appointed by three Governors, as Director of the 48th Agricultural District; serving in this position for twenty-two years.

In 1938 he was elected, President of the *Downey Chamber of Commerce,* and in 1940 he became the President of the *Kiwanis Club*. He held a seat as Director and Vice-President of *The Great Western Exhibition Center* in Los Angeles. He was also appointed to the Board of Directors of a new hospital being built in his city.

Above all of his accomplishments was his faith in God. He kept in mind where he came from. What resonated closely in his heart was his family's spiritual heritage. Never too busy for the things of God, he also served as lay minister of the *Full Gospel Armenian Church* of East Los Angeles. He was a tremendous support and financial backer of many ministries, evangelists, pastors, and missionaries. This was something Grandfather learned from his father and continued throughout his life as well.

It was beautiful to hear the spiritual blessing Great-Bobby received in 1955 when good-ol'-Magardich's grandson, Harry Mushegan had a vision. It happened at the *Armenian Pentecostal Church*. While standing close to Great-grandfather, Harry saw a bright light which came from Heaven and filled the church.

Then streams of oil began pouring over my great-grandfather's head. He was receiving a great Spiritual anointing!

My Great-Bobby Isaac's passing came on November 7, 1964. As he was reading the newspaper in bed, he peacefully passed away. He was 72 years old, and I was 5 years old.

A few weeks later on my sixth birthday, the Mayor of the City of Norwalk, Demetrio Apodaca signed "Resolution No.1337," which noted the passing of a Distinguished Citizen in the Los Angeles community, Mr. Isaac Shakarian.

All Great-Bobby, Isaac achieved couldn't match the faith he had in God.

He must be so happy being in the presence of the Lord. I can only presume how my Great-Bobby Isaac bubbled over with joy as he spoke to his Dad saying, *Did you see it, Dad? Did you see the words of the "Boy Prophet" back in Armenia came true when he prophesied, "Blessed will be the offspring of those who are in obedience; leaving their land and traveling to this new land [America], they will be a blessing to the nations. And now my son Demos is doing just that . . . blessing the nations!"*

Great-Bobby probably excitedly exclaimed, *it all came true!*

One of the last things Great-grandfather did before joining his father, mother and beloved wife in Heaven was to witness to a real estate broker about the love of the Lord. Later when this same broker and others were asked about Isaac Shakarian, their first words about him were always the same, "He was a man of God, a man of honor who deeply loved the Lord." You can say many things about my Great-Bobby, Isaac. He was a tremendous businessman, a major philanthropist, a huge backer of ministries and a caring man who never forgot his roots. Though all he achieved in his life couldn't match the faith he had in God.

THROUGH THE EYES OF OTHERS

My grandfather and his father were a dynamic team. Though both were humble men and known for their integrity. They were also greatly loved and highly esteemed in the community.

Great-Bobby and Bobby were alike in so many ways, but no more so than in their humanitarian efforts to help others. I'm sure both of them have received a huge reward in heaven for the support they gave to so many people worldwide, and their willingness to follow the voice of the Lord.

The *City of Downey* recognized Isaac with a "Commendation" for his Community Service and as a Community Leader.

The *Downey Board of Supervisors* adjourned holding a moratorium in honor of Isaac Shakarian.

The tributes continued to pour in from many who wanted to honor my Great-Bobby, Isaac including:

Edmond Brown, Governor of the State of California

Glenn M. Anderson, Lieutenant Governor of California

Evelle Younger, Judge from Los Angeles, California

Thomas Morton, Mayor in the City of Downey, California

There was also an overwhelming show of love from other businesses, pastors, evangelists, missionaries and many across the country.

Oral Roberts spoke at the Memorial honoring my great-grandfather Isaac saying, "Isaac stamped his family with his character, integrity of spirit and glorious faith in Jesus Christ. He became a force and a leading leader of men. Isaac was a

Alike in so many ways but no more so than in their humanitarian efforts to help others.

happy man filled with joy and kindness. He was very outgoing.
I loved him, and he loved me!"

> "Demos Shakarian was very instrumental in shaping my
> father, Roy's ministry after becoming a Spirit-filled Baptist
> Pastor along with Pastor John Osteen. One of my early
> memories as a child was at one of Demos' meetings held at
> the Shamrock Hilton Hotel in Houston, where Kenneth Hagin
> spoke. We were thrilled to see and hear of the moving of
> the Holy Spirit. Thank you Demos, for the powerful ministry
> that was our lifeline to the Spirit-filled ministry in the 1960's!"
>
> — **Larry Stockstill** • Pastor / Bethany World Prayer Center,
> Son of Roy Stockstill / Founder of Bethany Church

THE MILK PITCHER

My grandfather's organization continued to grow. Some
chapters experienced spontaneous growth, while others had to
persevere. He reminded the leadership in each city of a lesson he
had learned during the first year as he faced struggles. God had
told my grandfather to follow Him
and not to worry about anything else.
Adding, "That's what we learned at
Clifton's Cafeteria through the tests,
trials, and struggles we faced the first
year. God was faithful, and He brought the increase!"

*God was faithful
and He brought
the increase!*

My grandfather wanted to be very supportive helping
new chapters get established. One of my favorite adventures
Momie shared with me was when my grandparents had traveled to Lancaster, Pennsylvania, to encourage the opening of
a chapter.

Lancaster was primarily a farming community. They weren't sure about this organization for businessmen. Though, there was one man in Lancaster who desired to start a chapter in his town. Grandfather wanted to help him get it up and running, so he made a visit to explain about his organization. Of course, he also loved farmers so he was eager to assist in any way he could. He soon discovered it wasn't exactly an idea which the farmers embraced.

Nonetheless, a number of the farmers were invited to be the guests of my grandparents at a dinner, hosted by my grandfather. In an attempt to build rapport, my grand-

Milk spilled all over the front of his suit and ran down his cowboy boots!

father stood up and introduced himself as a fellow farmer. This announcement was met with silence. No one moved. They simply stared at him.

My grandmother always took her time describing the scene which followed. It was her favorite part of the story. "You know, Cynthia," she would say. "When your grandfather starts talking, he is accustomed to people hearing his heart. Well, that's not what happened this particular evening. The farmers just sat there and watched in silence, as your grandfather became increasingly nervous and more animated due to the lack of response."

"Finally, your grandfather opened his arms as wide as he could and drew them in as he said, 'The organization needs each one of us to participate!' And as he pulled his arms quickly toward his chest, he knocked over a pitcher of milk which was on the table."

This part of the story always brought her to laughter, and I could see the love she had in her heart for my grandfather. He was her best friend, and she adored every part of him. Still laughing, she would continue, "You should have seen your grandfather. The milk spilled all over the front of his suit and ran down his cowboy boots! He was so shocked by the accident with the milk pitcher, that without thinking he raised one foot on the table, boot and all. With milk still dripping off his boot, he started to clean his cowboy boot with the beautiful white-linen tablecloth, like he does when milk is spilled in the barn!"

He put his boot on the table. That's when we knew you are a real farmer!

I can still remember her sweet laughter as she repeated to me this story. "Cynthia, I couldn't believe my eyes that night! I said to him, 'Demos! What are you doing with that tablecloth?' Your grandfather was so embarrassed his face turned red! For a second he looked like he was taken aback by what I said."

Like the dairy farmer he is, he responded, "I am so sorry, old farmer habits die hard. My boots don't tell a lie. This sort of thing happens back in the barn milking cows all of the time. Any of you farmers here tonight ever had that happen? I certainly have, more times than I can count!"

Grandmother said she heard laughter coming from the back of the room. Then all of the farmers started laughing. Suddenly... they could relate. One farmer stood up and told how God had saved his crops that winter. Then another farmer shared how God brought rain when he desperately needed it. By the end of the evening, the new chapter was formed.

When we sang, 'His Banner Over Me is Love,' it was Demos Shakarian who showed it without restraint!

Grandmother always finished this story the same way, "That night was a blessing, but my favorite part was when your grandfather knocked that milk pitcher over! Oh, the look

We would sing 'Riding the Range for Jesus' for this true cowboy.

on his face! And you know what? I wasn't the only one.

Several of the farmers told your grandfather how much they loved his reaction when the milk spilled all over him and he put his boot on the table." They said, "That's when we knew you really are a farmer!"

"Demos Shakarian was 'A Man of Giant Faith.' The call of God on his life was a circle so big it included men from all walks of life. It was small beginnings at the first meetings, but the 'fire' was ignited. We met Demos and Rose at these meetings, and we became dear friends.

At his request, we would sing 'Riding the Range for Jesus' for this true cowboy. We never realized the day would come when the 'range' would be the whole world!

Under the leadership of Demos, men became dynamic leaders embracing the outpouring of the Holy Spirit. This 'platform' was one of the great factors in the Charismatic movement. The chapters and 'world conventions' became the events of the hour, and this platform launched many anointed ministries of the day.

I still honor this great man for making a place for my gift to be expanded; which began in the first chapter breakfasts at Clifton's Cafeteria and led to the largest convention centers throughout America.

Truly, when we sang, 'His Banner Over Me is Love,' it was Demos Shakarian who showed it without restraint!"

— Jerry and Sandi Barnard • Pastors / The Horizon Church

CHAPTER SIXTEEN

Start the Airlift Engines!

❦

*N*ow my grandfather's meetings and his vision was spreading worldwide and reaching a great variety of professions. I've highlighted just a hand full of the gatherings.

THE BILTMORE BOWL

In 1961, just nine years after my grandfather's organization began; Surgeon Dr. William Reed spoke to a crowd of over 1,500 at the *Biltmore Bowl* in Los Angeles. Many members of the medical profession were in attendance to hear how the Holy Spirit was impacting this Episcopalian physician's life.

In June 1963, Derek Prince, a former professor of Cambridge University, shared with Grandfather's organization in another standing room only meeting about when he was first filled with the Holy Spirit.

Pat Robertson, who received a Law degree from Yale University was the owner of many radio stations. This was before he became CEO of Regent University and Chairman of the Christian Broadcasting Network. He was an incredible catalyst for my grandfather's vision, as he re-broadcast Grandfather's conventions on his radio stations to the entire Northeastern United States. This brought tremendous growth and expansion.

THE AIRLIFTS TAKE OFF!

Now Grandfather was thinking even bigger and outside the box. He made a list of fifty countries to where he felt his organization needed to travel too. Large groups of members from Grandfather's organization all flew together to other countries, to spread God's love all over the world! This was when the Airlifts were birthed! At times there were hundreds and sometimes thousands of members who traveled together.

The "Airlifts" popularity grew, as many members wanted to be involved in spreading God's good news Internationally. Soon they were taking hundreds of people all over the world, including Africa and the Far East. In 1961 they went to Vietnam so members could pray with the soldier's right on the battlefield. Through the years there were Airlifts to many countries including Jerusalem, Egypt, Lebanon, and Puerto Rico. There was also a European-Scandinavian Airlift.

The "Airlifts" popularity grew spreading God's good news Internationally.

One of the highlights was a week-long event, which many members of the New Zealand chapters sponsored. The turnout was so big they had to rent a race track. Grandfather was thrilled to welcome everyone to Alexandra Park, in New Zealand!

LONDON HILTON HOTEL,
ROYAL ALBERT HALL & WESTMINSTER HALL

In 1965, over one-thousand members of Grandfather's organization and their families, chartered three SAS Jets and departed from Los Angeles, New York, and Chicago. All were arriving in

London. They were to attend meetings at the London Hilton Hotel, the Royal Albert Hall, and the Westminster Hall. These were three of the largest and most prestigious event venues in London. The convention opened with a Rally attended by 2,000 people, packing out Westminster Chapel. A prayer meeting was held the next morning in the Coronation Room of the London Hilton Hotel.

Everybody was absolutely amazed when the massive Royal Albert Hall holding 7,000 people, was filled to overflowing capacity. There were several thousand more standing outside unable to get a seat. My grandfather was told he would never be able to fill the Royal Albert Hall. On December 4, 1965, Grandfather filled it not once, but twice. First with young people and later with adults!

In addition, over 100,000 gospel tracts and pamphlets were handed out in the city. What a great move of the Holy Spirit as Oral Roberts led the final meeting, with Nicky Cruz leading the Youth Meetings. This was credited as one of the major influences of the Charismatic Renewal Movement in Britain.

Due to the success of the meetings in London, the members of my grandfather's organization spread out all over the globe evangelizing. They went to Israel, Italy, Rome, Scotland, Holland, Spain, France, Ireland, and Sweden, spreading the love of God. Many also went to Tokyo, Germany, Chile, Brazil, Bolivia, Finland, Hong Kong, Manila, Seoul, Venezuela, Peru, Norway, and Argentina. Now my grandfather was seeing the "Fulfillment of His Vision!"

ORAL ROBERTS & CHICAGO'S MAYOR

In 1965 there was excitement in the air, as Grandfather's World Convention was in Chicago. Held at the Conrad Hilton

Hotel, over four-thousand people crowded in the ballroom to hear guest speaker Oral Roberts. But first Richard J. Daley, the Mayor of Chicago, Illinois spoke. He addressed the crowd so powerfully saying, "We have problems in Chicago, but with the help of God we can overcome them. We need not only to have the love of God in our hearts, but love for others!"

THE SEALIFT

By 1975, Grandfather's organization had spread out again. When 160 members went to Nassau in the Bahamas, on the S.S. Emerald Seas.

Lives were being changed, as businessmen; some who would normally, not even attend a church service, was spreading God's love going to coffee shops, hotels and now even other countries.

Whether by planes, trains, automobiles, or now by boat, they were sharing their testimonies worldwide!

> "What we saw and what we want other people to know is that Demos Shakarian was used as a key component of a move of God which shook the nations. We saw it happen because we were there! The momentum and outreach of all these things were happening, and Demos was in the middle of it all. It was all part of the Charismatic movement. His ministry became a foundation of the movement.
>
> A humble man and an unlikely choice in man's eyes, God chose to use Demos to establish a new kind of ministry, which used ordinary men to take the gospel to the world. He was always so humble that people would see it's not about the big names. It's the humble spirit which God exalts.
>
> I watched Demos in services, he wasn't like any preacher

I knew. Other preachers would run out the back door when they finished preaching, but no, not Demos. He would stay and show love to everyone. Many times they would bring in homeless guys who were disheveled, and Demos would come and put his arms around them. That was Demos Shakarian!

Demos was a marvelous example 'to all of us,' and other ministers were so affected by him. We need more like him!

All the ministries of that day were affected somehow by Demos because he was always supporting other ministries. This included David Wilkerson who was on the streets of New York at this time. So likewise the people involved in the organization were doing the same thing because Demos was the one who was setting the example of building each other up. He was the best example anyone could have had. Demos and Rose also set an example through their marriage, and I know our marriage and many others benefited from watching them. Demos showed how a man should treat his wife, and Rose showed how a wife should respond to her husband and help him.

Demos could put his arms around those hurting and having a difficult time in their life. Then sit down with some of the outstanding businessmen of that time, including one of the Vice Presidents for the Chrysler Corporation. Demos attracted a lot of the top businessmen of the day. He would reach across all economic and social status, feeling just as comfortable with one group, as with another.

He could go into a meeting and just sit there not even saying anything. But he would change the focus of the meeting and the atmosphere, just by "his presence." It was a special anointing the Lord gave him.

I remember him saying; he told the Lord he would do whatever the Lord asked him to do. He was a great example for people to follow. So people can see what can be accomplished by those that turn their life over to the

Lord, as he did. Churches were accepting the businessmen involved with Demos Shakarian's organization in other

He would change the focus of the meeting and the atmosphere just by "his presence."

countries because they felt, the businessmen would help them in their country. They had different tour groups that went on "Airlifts." One went to England with about 3,000 people landing in London and fanned out all over Europe. We went with the group to Ireland and all over Europe spreading the Good News of the gospel.

In 1961, I heard the Lord say, 'Paul, would you go to Vietnam?' I met with Demos and a group of his men about going there to share the Lord. Thirty of us from his organization decided to go. A short time later we were on our way to Vietnam. We were staying in the Saigon Hotel and went to the Military Headquarters because we thought they could help us get around, but they wouldn't give us passage. They felt it would not be safe. So the men would go out into the streets and talk to the local soldiers and share about Jesus. But we were now stuck in just one place.

One very cold morning my roommate, Chuck Flynn, who we ministered with many times in the Prophetic meetings for Demos, said, "Come on Paul, let's kneel down and pray that God makes a way for us to start getting around Vietnam." Chuck prayed, and the next morning I got a call from Chaplain Merlin Carothers who said there was a Second Lieutenant with him. We immediately went to meet with him, and I told the Lieutenant our intentions to spread out to the hospitals and camps and talk to the boys. The Lieutenant said, "I can get you out of here. Just follow me." When the Major heard what we wanted to do, he gave "blank orders" so they could write in anywhere we wanted to go. The Lord gave us the whole nation, and it was like heaven just opened up to us. We were then able to fulfill our mission getting right where the boys were, on the battlefield!

This speaks to the average Christian, how the Lord has a job for them to do and He can open doors for them and promote them. Everything is converged, and right now God always has a leader. He always has someone he is raising up. And it is normally not the person you are looking at or the person you think it is going to be.

We want to ignite an understanding, that what this book, *The Shakarian Legacy* is about is so broad, and goes so beyond just what his organization did as a group of men. But how God used the obedience and the nature of the guy He put in charge of it, your grandfather. And how it affected the whole Christian world. He wanted to move in all the Spiritual gifts. When the Holy Spirit was moving, he didn't interfere or try to stop it; he let it move. It seemed like everything converged together at the right time.

It did more than play a part; it was actually like a wheel. There are many spokes of a wheel, but Demos was at the center of all of those spokes that enabled that wheel to roll!

All this is the bedrock of the future, and I believe your grandfather would say, "Yes, this was just the start and there is a freshness of the Holy Spirit and it's all over the world!" We have to have our eyes and ears open and not just feel like, this is the way it was. There is a second wind. It will break out and we have to have sensitivity to how the Spirit is going to do it.

It was the humility your grandfather displayed that exemplified the Holy Spirit. And the vision is still alive today. Demos always saw a person as more than what they were. He had a very wonderful gift. He would see in people what they didn't see in themselves and then they would begin to catch a vision of what they could be!"

— **Paul and Joyce Toberty** • Authors / *A Nation Born in a Day*

CHAPTER SEVENTEEN

And That's How
My Bobby Rolled!

❦

his great move of the Holy Spirit was certainly not done by one man alone. It could only have been accomplished through the power of God. It was the key reason why Grandfather sought the Lord for direction in everything he did.

My grandfather had an ear to hear the Lord. When someone asked him, "Demos, did you know how big your organization would become?" His answer was always the same. "No, I would just listen and follow His direction."

That God used a dairy farmer to start a worldwide businessman's organization can be easily summed up; man looks at the outside appearance, but God looks at the heart! It's the humble heart that God exults.

> "I feel like I grew up in Demos Shakarian's meetings. My parents, Joe and Linda Ninowski, Sr. were intimate friends of the Shakarians and our families shared memorable times through the years. My father was an International Director of Demos' organization. I remember many Saturday morning breakfast meetings at the Skippers Table Restaurant in Detroit, watching and experiencing the power of God's love transform people's lives. They say more is caught than taught — and I gleaned so much being in the atmosphere of the ministry that Demos birthed.

Whenever you were with Demos Shakarian, you could sense an uncompromising, immovable Godly character and feel his genuine love for people. This love fueled his passion for bringing the life-changing message of hope to the world. He achieved this by building a beautiful bridge of friendship. He created a dialog with the leaders of commerce and leaders of nations. Demos' warm and weathered voice reflected his seasoned trust in God. A trust which was learned, from a lifetime of hard work and many mountains climbed.

There may be no greater testament to a person's life than to see Their Vision Continue and Their Mission Outlive Them!

That has been evidenced by Cynthia Shakarian taking the baton that Demos passionately carried and bringing the message to a new generation, with relevance and a compelling new voice. The world is a better place for having had Demos Shakarian in it.

I am honored to have known him and to have been immeasurably influenced by his life. Next to my father, whom I consider the greatest man I've ever known, Demos Shakarian stood right there alongside him!"

— Joe Ninowski, Jr • Daystar Television Network / Producer, Music Director, Writer

FIDEL CASTRO

My grandparents flew to Cuba and checked into the Havana Hilton, which had been renamed the *Cuba Libre*. Fidel Castro had recently taken charge over Cuba. My grandparents were surprised to hear that not only was he over Cuba but this hotel was now his headquarters.

Late one night my grandfather was preparing to retire when he suddenly felt the prompting he knew so well. Being led by the Holy Spirit, he dressed quickly to go downstairs. Grandmother heard him moving around the room and asked, "What are you doing, Demos?" While finishing getting dressed, my grandfather explained he believed he was supposed to meet Fidel Castro. "Meet with Fidel Castro!" she questioned? As she laid her head back on the pillow, she knew that God was leading him.

As he made his way down, he noticed guards armed with machine guns. He cautiously sat down, being alone in the coffee shop. The waiter and my grandfather began to converse as best they could, due to the language barrier. The waiter asked, "Señor, how can I help you? Will someone be joining you?" Removing his Stetson hat, he answered, "No, just a cup of coffee, por favor."

> *You can get so busy with what you're expected to do, you can easily miss what you were born to do!*

As the waiter placed the coffee on the table, my grandfather looked up and asked him, "Have you seen Fidel Castro? Do you know when he will be coming in the restaurant?" The waiter replied, "Premier Castro doesn't come at night." Grandfather looked at the waiter and said, "Oh, he will. My source is never wrong!" The waiter's eyes grew large, and he leaned forward and whispered, "Do you have privileged information?" "Yes, you could say someone told me he would be here," my grandfather responded. The waiter mumbled under his breath while shaking his head, "This man is loco!"

Finishing his coffee, Grandfather stood up to leave and heard footsteps echoing on the tile floor. Heavily armed soldiers entered with Fidel Castro. The soldiers took their positions around the room as Castro sat down and ordered

My father and I have built one of the largest dairies in the world starting with only three cows and a prayer.

a meal. When the waiter finished taking his order, he leaned over and whispered into Castro's ear. Castro stared directly at my grandfather, motioning for Grandfather to join him.

He and Castro spoke for over a half hour. Fidel Castro asked my grandfather, "Why are you here in Cuba?" Grandfather replied, "I am a simple Armenian-American dairyman. My father and I have built one of the largest dairies in the world; starting with only three cows and a prayer."

"My desire is to learn the way of the people here and the way of the land. We have come to Cuba not only to learn the culture, but to learn how the Holy Spirit is leading Cubans in their businesses and their daily lives." The soldiers leaned in and watched my grandfather, while their guns followed his every move. Yet, Castro seemed interested and my grandfather was thrilled he had an opportunity to share the Lord with him. Grandfather asked, "May I pray for your country and the leaders?" After conversing, he thanked Grandfather for coming to Cuba and especially for praying for the people of Cuba. Then getting up, he extended his hand to Grandfather while they said their goodbyes.

Upon returning to his room, he shook the bed calling out Grandmother's name, "Rose, Rose! I met him! I told you, Fidel Castro!" Rose smiled at him, knowing her husband has an ear to hear. Traveling internationally, my grandparents met many world leaders and heads of state in countries they visited. They were able to share God's love and pray for them, as he did with Fidel Castro.

ROOM 317

What a blessing it was, to see so many clergies from the Catholic denomination at my grand-father's meetings. Many would not attend an evangelical church, but felt free to attend in a hotel ballroom or private meeting room. Just like what happened on that very special night in South Bend, Indiana on March 13th, 1967.

How could a room in the administration building at the University of Notre Dame become the most historic room?

How could a room in the administration building at the University of Notre Dame become one of the most historic rooms? Room 317 was that room!

"In 1967 an awakening which would shake the globe began with a prayer meeting amongst hungry young people. It was a Monday evening, March 13th. My grandfather Roy Wead who was the pastor of one of the largest Protestant churches in South Bend, Indiana received a call from one of his deacons, Ray Bullard. He informed Granddad of a prayer meeting which was about to take place that evening. Ray had been contacted by a professor from the University of Notre Dame, about a group of Catholic graduate students and associate professors at Notre Dame. They were searching to know more about Jesus.

Ray and Mabel Bullard were the leaders of the local chapter of Demos Shakarian's organization, in South Bend. They welcomed those from the University of Notre Dame who wanted to join them. The Holy Spirit began to move during the prayer meeting, and nine of the students and teachers experienced the gift of tongues.

Soon the meetings were held at the University of Notre Dame campus, so many more students and faculty could attend. They met in the administration building, Room 317!

Through that room, the continuation of the move of the Holy Spirit overflowed throughout the campus. People flew in from around the world, and the testimony of what God was doing at Notre Dame spread swiftly. Within weeks, other campuses across the United States began to see similar outpourings.

Fifty years after that evening in South Bend, the Catholic Charismatic Renewal still exists in over 230 countries, with over 160 million members. Demos Shakarian was the forerunner who had the courage, wisdom, and insights to not only take the gospel outside the four walls of the church but to also, break down denominational boundaries. The results have been a spiritual bonanza!"

— **Scott Wead** • Pastor / Life House Worship Center

KENNETH HAGIN, FRED PRICE & JOHN OSTEEN

Meetings and conventions were being held continuously around the world. My grandfather loved attending as many as he could. I wouldn't be surprised if he was on a first name basis with everyone at the airport! Though all the meetings are worth mentioning, I've featured just a few.

In 1976 a Regional Convention was held at the Sheraton Waikiki in Honolulu, Hawaii. My grandfather was thrilled to welcome everyone along with speakers, Kenneth E. Hagin and Frederick K. C. Price.

Later that summer of 1976, the World Convention was at the Americana Hotel in Miami Beach, Florida. Television personality Graham Kerr spoke along with Pat Boone, T. L. Osborn, and Actor Dean Jones.

The World Convention held in July 1979 took place in New Orleans. Thousands listened intently as John Osteen shared, "We have the power of the Holy Spirit moving in us. When we begin to move out, we cause God to go into action. We must not hide the Glory of God. The World is in need of what God has done!"

In October 1979, Ralph Sariejo had been filled with the Holy Spirit and shared his experience with my grandfather's organization. He was a Production Manager for the television series "McMillan and Wife," becoming a producer for "The Bionic Woman" TV series, and a producer on "Salvage 1" with Andy Griffith. Gaining a reputation for working creatively and within the budget, he gave all the credit to trusting in God and letting HIM completely guide his professional life.

> "Personally, my closest encounter with Demos Shakarian happened in the mid-1980s. I had just finished speaking at Kenneth Copeland's Believer's meeting in Anaheim, California. Demos sent word he would like to have lunch with me. At the restaurant, he moved quickly to his reasons for asking me. He said he felt I was a spiritual person and would be able to understand his heart.
>
> Demos Shakarian impacted the lives of my husband and myself greatly. We were among the people swept up in the Charismatic Move who ventured outside our denominational walls, and this was largely due to Demos Shakarian's ministry."
>
> — **Billye Brim** • Founder / Billye Brim Ministries,
> Prayer Mountain in the Ozarks

KENNETH COPELAND & ANDRE CROUCH

The first time I heard Kenneth Copeland speak was at one of my grandfather's conventions, in a youth meeting. Little did I know the powerful influence he and his precious wife Gloria would end up having in my life. I will never forget looking around and seeing so many adults attending the "Youth" event! People loved his message, and it didn't take long before he soon became the speaker in the main auditorium.

Andrae Crouch had the same power. Back then they were known as *Andrae Crouch and the Disciples*. Their spirit-led music was awesome. Andrae found joy in everything, continually joking as a group of us would go out to eat. Though it was his anointed music which touched me so powerfully.

"Growing up I spent a lot of time with my grandparents, A.W. and Vinita Copeland. Their house was FULL of Jesus. Everything reflected Him. I absorbed all I could especially in my elementary school years during the '60s. One thing I always relied on was the Voice Magazine, a product of Demos Shakarian's ministry. I would scoop it up and go through it page by page. When I was very young, the pictures are what drew me. As I grew older, it was the stories of salvation, and how the power of the Holy Spirit in people's lives had changed everything!

Later on, I had the amazing privilege of attending Demos' International Convention, with Oral Roberts and Kathryn Kuhlman in the main auditorium. Kenneth E. Hagin and Kenneth Copeland (my dad) spoke in the youth meeting, with Andrae Crouch doing the music!

I do not exaggerate when I say the power could be felt in the parking lot! Millions of people worldwide have the same kind of testimony I have because of Demos Shakarian. He knew the

I do not exaggerate when I say the power could be felt in the parking lot!

power of the Holy Spirit and proved it, as he made way for the move of the Spirit on a level that America and the world had never seen!

He was a man of The Word and The Spirit!"

— **Terri Copeland Pearsons** • Senior Pastor / Eagle Mountain Church

VOICE MAGAZINE

When my grandfather's organization began to publish *Voice Magazine*, it grew rapidly in popularity. They desired to relate to everyone regardless of anyone's affiliation. So they begin printing one magazine for the Presbyterians, one for the Catholics, the Church of Christ, the Baptists, Attorneys, Lawmen, Military, and so on. They would gear it towards what was happening in their religion or field of business. The chapters or even individuals would pay for certain denominations. This included one for the University of Notre Dame, which was a cornerstone for the release of the Holy Spirit in many denominations. This also came out of a chapter from Grandfather's organization.

PRESIDENT DUVALIER IN HAITI

My grandfather helped millions of people around the world, including nations like Haiti. Because of his humanitarian efforts, Grandfather received an invitation from President Francois Duvalier known as Papa Doc. He readily accepted the invitation because he was concerned about how the Haitians were being treated. He had found favor with President Duvalier and was granted permission to hold three weeks of meetings there.

This was the inception of Grandfather's organization starting the *Airlifts* to other countries. There were twenty-five members from his organization, representing different walks of life that joined my grandparents on this historic trip to Haiti. As his organization spread rapidly, Grandfather then began to understand; it would be the *Airlifts* which would allow him to reach the world.

To honor Grandfather, there was a motorcade escort consisting of military motorcyclist. Trailing them were several black stately limousines, which took my grandparents to the Riviera Hotel. The three weeks of meetings which he was given permission for; was held at *The Sylvio Cato Stadium* in Port-au-Prince. The stadium held 23,000 people, but up to 35,000 a night were arriving to attend. In attendance were also many Government Officials, Senators, and Generals seated on the platform.

During the meeting, red-hooded voodoo priests were chanting and coercing others to join them to come against my grandfather. The guards aimed their rifles towards the priests, but Grandfather saw this and immediately raised his hand to the guard and signaled them to wait. As he quickly closed his eyes and prayed for the Lord's intervention.

There was incredible tension in the auditorium, and unrest appeared to overtake the place. Everything seemed to stand still when they heard a man from the midst began to yell out, "He can see, he can see! Oh my God! My boy can see!"

Grandfather than began to understand it would be the Airlifts which would allow him to reach the world!

My grandfather looked around to see where the voice was coming from. Emerging from the crowd and rushing up to the platform, was a tall man with a boy trailing him. Grandfather asked,

"What do you mean?" And as the man began to share about this incredible healing there was a roar of applause as people realized, God had given this little blind boy sight.

Men, women, and children began rushing towards the platform wanting to know more about the God who healed this boy, who was known in the town to be blind. Thousands

"May I pray for your country and its leaders?"

were weeping with hands lifted high while accepting the Lord in their hearts. The next day Grandfather reflected on the meetings, thanking the Lord for all the people who were blessed.

Prior to leaving, Grandfather met with President Duvalier in the Presidential Palace asking the question he would ask every government official he met. Which was, "May I pray for your country and its leaders?" President Duvalier nodded in response and requested Grandfather, to specifically pray for desperately needed rain for his country. Everyone in the room bowed their heads as Grandfather prayed.

The next day . . . it poured! Grandfather's prayer was answered.

A MAN OF HONESTY AND INTEGRITY

My Bobby took his role as the leader of his organization very seriously and with integrity. He knew he was responsible for the welfare and the protection of his members within the organization. He also greatly respected the call on his life. It was not always an easy decision, but to Grandfather, his choice was sure. God always came first. He knew if he didn't stay honest to the anointing, his organization would never reach its full potential.

"The first time I met Demos Shakarian was sometime after the movie and the book release of, "The Cross and the Switchblade." I immediately saw then what a humble man he was and that he was a very smart businessman too!

> *I observed how he would carefully separate himself from anything that was not in line with God's word.*

It was through Demos that I made my first trip to London in the early '70s. I spoke with him at the Royal Albert Hall for a youth event, and that place was packed. I then traveled with him many times and in every convention, the crowds overflowed where we ministered!

I observed how he would carefully separate himself from anything that was not in line with God's word — and not good for his ministry.

He had such a heart for the Gospel and was a missionary to the business world. In spite of leading an extremely busy life, he managed to maintain his balance in the midst of everything.

Recently I had the privilege to speak to three-thousand men in Armenia, and I thought of Demos Shakarian. I thank God for using him in such a powerful way. I fell in love with the Armenian people. I saw how much they respected Demos Shakarian and the great impact he has had on them."

— **Nicky Cruz** • Nicky Cruz Outreach,
Subject of *The Cross and the Switchblade*

GRAND OLE OPRY STARS

A USA Convention in the summer of 1984 was held in Nashville, Tennessee. There were testimonies and special appearances by many Grand Ole Opry Stars, including Charlie Daniels and Jeannie Riley, known for her pop hit *Harper Valley PTA*.

Speakers included my grandfather, Ben Kinchlow a host of *The 700 Club*, Sam Moore an R & B singer-songwriter, Mark

Rutland who became the 3rd President of Oral Roberts University, and Charles Osborn who was T.L. Osborn's father. They all shared how the power of God moved in their lives.

My grandfather always recruited a spiritual powerhouse lineup! Looking back at the great speakers and singers at those conventions I remember thinking *how can I choose which meeting to attend?* As the youth meetings were just as powerful as the meetings in the main auditoriums. I wanted to hear them all!

KIM CLEMENT

On June 27, 2015, I attended one of Kim Clement's meetings. He asked me to stand up and began speaking to me personally about my grandfather. After graciously welcoming me, he explained he was in the ministry because of my grand-

My grandfather always recruited a spiritual powerhouse lineup!

father. He said, "I wanted you to see how far your grandfather's ministry reached, to a very, very small town in South Africa, where no one believed in me. I was rejected." The next week he explained his story to me in more detail.

"I found Christ in the street after years of drug abuse and addictions. It was during those moments while facing death, I heard for the first time in my life the voice of God. It wasn't loud sounding, but rather something that entered the deepest part of my spirit. And within seconds I received the knowledge of God.

I was instructed to give my music to Him, surrender my soul and begin a journey which would take me to the world. I was called by God to serve Him in ministry, but having no church background whatsoever; I sought to find what this meant through a Bible Study group in a local Pentecostal church.

After a few months of seeking for answers and direction, a local chapter of Demos' organization sought a pianist to lead songs before the special guest would speak. I had no idea what this organization was about, but would over the years build a strong relationship with them. However, this night I had no idea because of my participation in this event; God would reach down and breathe on me, and launch me into full-time ministry.

As the guest evangelist Pastor Fred Roberts from Durban preached so powerfully, the Spirit of the Lord swept through the building and rested upon me. For the first time, I began to play music I had never rehearsed or performed before. I started singing words I'd never sung before. As this began happening, the evangelist, Fred Roberts swung around and declared, 'God's Spirit is on you and has instructed me to release an anointing on you to prophesy on the piano, and sing His Song!'

Something fell on me, and I felt like I had been raised up to a higher place. As I sang and ministered which I had never done previously, it was in the atmosphere that Demos Shakarian had released from his beginnings, and I was released into ministry. The evangelist didn't continue but released me to conduct the entire meeting, which I did with ease. Demos always anticipated God's presence to touch the lives of hardened men and women, and this night was no exception.

I had always heard of the freedom and liberty of the Holy Spirit desired by Demos Shakarian. I was privileged to meet him many years later. While seated at a restaurant in Orange County, California. I slowly and cautiously moved out of my seat towards him, and he turned and looked at me and said, 'I know.' It was one of those moments I will never forget. With tears in my eyes, I said, 'Thank you. It was because of your vision

Your grandfather's ministry reached, to a very, very small town in South Africa!

that I am here today.' He replied with a sparkle in his eye, 'I know.'

I attribute my initial separation into ministry to the great mantle which rested on Demos Shakarian. From that point, I attended and ministered at many of Demos' meetings and with his son, Richard throughout South Africa and the USA.

Demos Shakarian touched his generation in such a massive way. What is so amazing to me is his vision never died, but affected so many all over the world. The truth will reverberate through many generations to come!"

— Kim Clement • Kim Clement Center / Musician and Prophet /
Helped countless numbers of people in need including
many children with special needs

CHAPTER EIGHTEEN

A Dream Fulfilled

At 21 years old, my Real Estate career was growing fast which allowed me to purchase my dream car; a candied apple red 945 Porsche and my first investment property. I was feeling on top of the world!

It felt like I had come a long way from the pink pajama wearing eight-year-old little girl, or the fifteen-year-old Cher wanna be! I found myself sitting in my grandfather's office chair at his International Headquarters, looking at all the pictures hanging on the wall. Even though I always felt the love my grandfather gave me, these photos captured the love he showed towards humanity.

INCREASING

Even his International Headquarters had come together by once again, the Lord blessing whatever my grandfather put his hand to.

Grandfather purchased a large plot of land in Costa Mesa, California, which fronted the 405 Freeway. When he originally purchased it, there was only a small shopping center across the road. He eventually built the International Headquarters on this property. Not long after that *South Coast Plaza,* the shopping center across the freeway became the largest mall on the West Coast, and one of the most famous and luxurious shopping centers in California!

This replaced my grandfather's original International Headquarters on Figueroa Street in downtown Los Angeles.

THE NEW INTERNATIONAL HEADQUARTERS

The Dedication of Grandfather's International Headquarters was on January 27, 1980. Oral Roberts led the ceremony of the state-of-the-art building, and Pat Boone was the emcee. Oral Roberts reminisced with Grandfather about the first meeting he had, when only eighteen people showed up. Remarking, "Wow! Look what God has done!" Words of Congratulations poured in, including from the current President of the United States, Jimmy Carter and the President of Egypt, Anwar Sadat.

Grandfather held Advanced Leadership Training Seminars. It drew people from around the world.

The construction of this building cost 5 million dollars. It was spectacularly designed by Architect, Joel Colombo, and is one of the most beautiful modern buildings I have ever seen. All three stories of the 65,000 square foot building had a purpose. The 125 employees were excited to be a part of the vision; to spread God's love to businesses and in marketplaces around the globe.

In this facility, Grandfather also held *Advanced Leadership Training Seminars.* People flew in from around the world to come under his teaching on how to reach their community for Christ.

"Years ago I operated an automobile sales and leasing company. I was successful and making money, but something was missing in my life. While I was trying to figure out what that was, I reflected back to my teenage years. It was during that time my father, Dr. Irvine Harrison was hired as the first executive secretary of Demos Shakarian's organization. In that capacity, he decided to take my mother and me to several of Demos' conventions.

It was at these conventions; I was made aware of a different kind of successful businessman. These men were making money but had a greater purpose to their lives. They were active in their church, involved in missions and helping needy people worldwide.

One night I said, 'I want what these men have.' Within twenty-four hours I was at Demos' World Convention in San Francisco.

The following day with tears flowing, I prayed for God's Spirit to reside and empower my life in a new and fresh way. Soon I began to share my testimony at chapters around California, then across America. A teaching gift began to emerge, and soon doors at some of the world's largest churches and in the secular world began to open. Since then I have traveled worldwide sharing Biblical keys to increase.

I am just one of scores of teachers and ministers who owe an eternal debt of gratitude to Demos Shakarian. Because of him, we continue to impact people's lives across the globe!"

— Bob Harrison • Founder / Increase

AND THE EMMY AWARD GOES TO . . .

In the 1970's, Grandfather was ready to take the next step in bringing the good news of Jesus Christ to as many people as

> *"After all,*
> *I'm a dairyman not*
> *a television star!"*

he could, but especially to the general public. The best way he knew to do this was to start a television show he called, *Good News.*

He put together many prime-time specials called, "Good News America" and "Turning Point." As you can imagine, now with the continual media attention, my grandfather was having a profound effect on not only the general public but on World Leaders.

Though my Bobby quickly discerned filming for television was an experience very foreign to him. In front of a camera, he was like a "fish out of the water!" Grandfather was not comfortable at all, a fact he came to realize when he filmed the first few *Good News* television programs.

As the host, Grandfather would be given a script which he was supposed to follow. This was not exactly how Grandfather worked. He always spoke from his heart, and his message came out perfectly. When he had a script, the flow, and the anointing was not there!

After all, "I'm a dairyman, not a television star," he would say. Having to read from a script in front of the camera and television crew, was an entirely foreign experience.

Grandfather would laugh as he told me how the sweat would pour down his face because he was so nervous. It didn't take long for him to realize, reading from a script was simply not going to work. He started filming the programs as God directed him. He would pray before the filming and God took care of the rest!

Everyone was amazed, even without a script Grandfather would wrap up the program exactly on time, every time. When he was finished, he would give all the Glory to God.

He greatly appreciated his son Steve, who offered his creativity and was a key to these shows becoming a success. Using his talents, he produced the majority of these programs. Uncle Steve was also incredibly gifted musically and had a God-given talent to play the trumpet.

In fact in High School, he formed a band with a couple of fellow students who were brother and sister; Karen and Richard Carpenter.

He reached out to bring much needed help and unity.

The Carpenter family lived close to my grandparents in Downey. Karen and Richard became known as *The Carpenters!* They were one of the biggest-selling music artists of all time, with many hits including, *We've Only Just Begun.*

One of my grandfather's television specials, "Good News America" also made its mark in history, when the program won – an Emmy Award!

> "Though I only had the privilege of enjoying a meal with Demos on one occasion, his life and ministry had a genuine impact on my life. His example of listening to and following the voice of the Holy Spirit was inspiring. I am personally acquainted with a number of men whose lives were also changed by God through the ministry of Demos Shakarian. Only eternity will truly reveal the extent of all that was accomplished through the life of this servant of God!"
> — **Bayless Conley** • Pastor / Cottonwood Church

A HUMANITARIAN

His entire life, Grandfather never forgot the people in Armenia, or the fact that this is where his roots originally started. He helped numerous people there and many others in need around the globe. Grandfather didn't hesitate to step-in and help individuals, flying in medical sup-plies and necessities for their daily needs, including in nations like Haiti.

Can you imagine what this world would be like, if we all encouraged each other in this way?

Grandfather worked with many Humanitarian groups sending aid to famine victims. He reached out to bring much-needed help and unity, working with a variety of other countries as well.

> "Annie and I had the privilege of visiting the Shakarians' in their home in Downey, California. As soon as we walked into the living room and met Demos, we were struck by the unmistakable witness of the presence and anointing of the Lord. We knew we were meeting with one of God's Generals.
>
> Demos was undoubtedly 'one-of-a-kind.' He was a coordinator and facilitator par excellence, in spreading the full gospel message to almost every corner of the globe.
>
> Only eternity will tell all the individuals and nations that have been blessed directly and indirectly through this humble, yet outstanding servant of the Lord. We bless his memory!"
>
> **— Ken and Annie Schisler** • Face To Face Ministry

AN ENCOURAGER AND A LOYAL FRIEND

I've heard, God uses ordinary people to do extraordinary things! Well, that might explain how God took a dairyman who did not like to talk to large groups of people and gave him a platform that reached around the world. He was a man who didn't only speak about God's love but showed it by loving and encouraging others.

My grandfather had an incredible gift to see people as *more than* they were. It was not just puffing people up. He was known to actually see people like they didn't see themselves. Then they would begin to catch the vision of what they could be.

Can you imagine what this world would be like if we all encouraged each other in this way?

People were continually trying to give Grandfather honorary degrees, but he always said, "No, that's not who I am." He would say jokingly, "As soon as I would open my mouth they will know I am not a doctor! I'm just a dairy farmer, a helper."

His example encouraged others to trust the Lord to open doors for them and to use their gifts, just as he had.

Grandfather stayed faithful to the vision God had given him. He was completely transparent. What you saw was what you got. A Stetson-wearing dairy farmer, who loved his cows, his family, and friends, but above all loved his Lord and Savior.

"Demos Shakarian made a huge impact in New York City. The yearly conventions brought great speakers like Kathryn Kuhlman, Oral Roberts, and Kenneth Hagin. Thousands had encounters with God and witnessed the power of God through miracles.

My father, Simon Vikse, and Demos became very close friends during their national travels and Airlifts to Europe, sharing the Good News with businessmen. His visits to New York were a highlight to my family and church because Demos always had fresh, inspirational stories of what God was doing around the world.

Demos Shakarian was authentic in his pursuit of God and in his relationships with friends.

When my dad passed away, Demos flew in from a convention in Hawaii to New York, almost five-thousand miles away, to be at the funeral.

A testimony to Demos Shakarian's love, his friendship, and his loyalty!"

— **Arlene Vikse Del Rio** • Pastor / Abounding Grace Ministries, New York

HIS VISION KEPT GROWING

The weekly radio program was now in 21 different languages, throughout Europe, Asia, and South America. Now the weekly *Good News* television program was broadcast nationally. Grandfather's goal was to reach 1 billion, 250 million people.

It didn't take long before other countries were adding the half-hour show to their lineup, including Canada, Australia, and Japan. It was televised on 150 stations and reached almost 123 million people by the mid-1970s. His dream was becoming a reality as doors continued to open worldwide.

By 1976 around twenty-five years after the first meeting at Clifton's Cafeteria, there were thousands of chapters around the world. Several times a year his organization continued to sponsor Airlifts to other countries, and subscriptions to their magazine grew to 800,000 subscribers. My grandfather had now flown well over two-million miles fulfilling his purpose in life!

"I heard about Demos' mighty vision God had given him, and I've seen the Lord bless his obedience in doing it.

It's One Thing to Have a Great Vision and another to Obey the Vision!! He leaves behind a great heritage. He was truly a great man of God. His vision will go on until the coming of the Lord. All Glory to our Lord!"

— **Glenda Jackson** • Niece of Maria Woodworth-Etter, Glenda Jackson Ministries

JOEL OSTEEN

What I learned most from my Bobby was to press on and not give up on the desires of my heart. He continued to trust that he was in the center of God's will. This is a message

People don't determine your destiny, God does!

he loved to pass on to people who came to him discouraged with the direction their life was taking.

I would hear him encouraging others to keep their focus and attention on God; and to never, ever give up! It reminded me of one of my favorite messages from Joel Osteen.

"It's not important how you start out in your life but how you finish. Recondition your mind. Don't let the negative things which have happened in your family or in your life be passed down to the next generation. You Can Be The Difference Maker!

You can be the one who sets a course of honoring God, a course of favor, of honor, and victory!

Get rid of strongholds which are holding you back. God is a progressive God. He wants every generation to increase. Stir up the seeds of greatness God put in you. You are supposed to go further than the generation before you. You can overcome obstacles and break down barriers.

Don't let what others say about you hold you back.

People don't determine your destiny, God does! Stay in faith and instead of defeating you; it will propel you.

God knows how to take what was meant for your harm and use it to your advantage. You will see your dreams come to pass, and become everything God created you to be!"

THE DIFFERENCE MAKER!

I see this is what my Bobby did. He would not give up until he knew for certain that he had fulfilled the purpose he was put on this earth for.

He overcame many obstacles and endured some negative feedback by those who didn't understand his vision. Yes, my Bobby was steadfast in pursuing his purpose by following the only voice that really mattered . . . God's!

"Calvary Chapel Downey was meeting at the Downey Civic Center on Sunday mornings. The church entered a period of explosive growth. I told God 'He would have to do something!' So I began praying. A friend of mine told me to go over and take a look at the old 'White Front store building,' saying 'It's the only one locally bigger than what we have now.' This was a 150,000 square-foot building on a 12-acre lot.

I made some inquiries and found out Demos Shakarian owned the property. I called him to set up a meeting. I liked Demos immediately. He was a good-natured man who treated everyone as a friend. But he was also a good businessman.

I shared with Demos, we were interested in leasing a portion of the building for our church services. He replied he was not interested in leasing, but we should buy it. He gave us an incredible opportunity on a prime spot. Demos said he believed this land was ours explaining, he had dedicated it to God and he wanted God's business to take place there. After much prayer, the papers were signed and Calvary Chapel of Downey took over the building. On Easter Sunday 1978 our first service was held, and the rest is history. Thanks to Demos who dedicated this land to God and encouraged us to buy it, and thanks be to God who made it all happen. To God be the glory!"

— **Jeff Johnson** • Pastor / Calvary Chapel Downey

THE ATHLETES

Grandfather always tried to find an avenue to expand the Kingdom of God. Like he did the Hollywood sect, the Political arena, and as he began to do with the Athletes of the day. He knew the athletes were heroes to many, and they would be a strong influence in the country.

Tom Landry, the coach of the Dallas Cowboys said Grandfather's organization made a big impression on him!

A few who shared with my grandfather's organization were Orel Hershiser, the only baseball player to receive the Cy Young Award, the Championship Series MVP Award, and the World Series MVP Award in the same season. Also, Allen Rice, former professional football player, who played running back for eight seasons for the Minnesota Vikings and the Green Bay Packers.

Tom Landry, the incredible coach of the Dallas Cowboys, also made a big impression on my grandfather's organization.

And Coach Landry explained, *my grandfather's organization made a big impression on him!*

Grandfather reached many athletes from almost every sport so they could testify about their faith and trust in God!

> "Cynthia, your granddad Demos Shakarian was a great leader. He got businessmen involved in the ministry, which eventually went around the world. I remember Josh McDow and I drove to meet Demos at his office, and he was the kindest man.
>
> Millions of people have been blessed because of your granddad. I am proud to say I am one of them. I got to speak at many of his meetings, and I was amazed wherever we went they were always full, and everyone was so encouraging. You should be proud, and I know you are of your wonderful granddad!"
>
> — **Roosevelt (Rosey) Grier** • All-Pro New York Giants who played five World Championship Games, member of NFL's "Fearsome Foursome" / Helped apprehend the gunman who assassinated Robert F. Kennedy at the Ambassador Hotel

SINGING COWBOYS

The meetings had attracted people from all fields of life including Johnny Cash, Roy Rodgers, and Pat Boone, who spoke at the Americana Hotel in Miami, Florida. Even Dale Evans was a speaker in one of the women's meetings.

It's been said if my grandfather was sitting in a meeting, it would change the atmosphere just by his presence. It was a special anointing the Lord gave him!

> "In 1984 I spoke at Demos' International Convention in Anaheim. It was a powerful service, and the Holy Spirit was

moving on people to really love God and one another. A message that Demos lived!"

— **James Robison** • Founder / LIFE Outreach International / Host of *Life Today*

CHAPTER NINETEEN

The White House Takes Notice

≈≈≈

In 1977 my grandfather was invited by President Jimmy Carter to represent him at a ceremony in Egypt. Grandfather was known as a man who *promoted peace* and *goodwill*. His good reputation had reached The White House.

AN AMBASSADOR

He considered it a great honor to meet with the President of the United States and represent him, and our country. This invitation allowed him to meet with President Anwar Sadat.

Presidents and Heads of State from other countries began to invite Grandfather to meet with them as well. He was sought after for his *excellent skills in negotiation; encouraging unity* and *kindness to all.* As he always did, Grandfather also shared the love of God with everyone. Many did not only meet with him, but they also prayed with him.

A SPECIAL INVITATION

There were many conventions held throughout the world by the 1980's. Although once a year in July, thousands of members would come together with representatives from all of the chapters worldwide, for my grandfather's International Convention. What a beautiful site it was to see. People from all religions, all races, and nationalities, worshiping the Lord together just like my Bobby saw in his vision.

The World Convention in the summer of 1982, was the 30th Anniversary of my grandfather's organization. It was held at the *Anaheim Convention Center* in Anaheim, California. It proved to be exciting as Dr. Paul Y. Cho from South Korea delivered an incredible message, as did Kenneth Copeland and Jack Hayford.

In July of 1983, the annual International Convention was held at the *Cobo Center* in Detroit, Michigan. Kenneth Copeland spoke the first night with Kenneth Hagin speaking the following evening. Both nights the attendance had an overflowing crowd.

During this convention right before Kenneth Copeland was to speak, my Bobby made an exciting announcement. The White House had called requesting my grandfather to come to Washington D.C. the following week because President Ronald Reagan was seeking to meet with him. As everyone in the auditorium erupted with joy and stood to their feet, my Bobby immediately brought the attention back to the members of his organization. He was never boastful about what the Lord was doing through his life. He knew he was a willing vessel who desired to please God while he was on this earth.

PRESIDENT RONALD REAGAN

The 31st International Convention in July of 1984 was again held at the *Anaheim Convention Center* in Anaheim, California.

It was a wonderful surprise for the thousands of people who

packed the Convention Center, to hear that current President Ronald Reagan had sent a videotaped "special greeting" for the members of Grandfather's organization. Paul and Jan Crouch, founders of Trinity Broadcasting Network was at the convention filming the event, as they had done the previous year. So the President's greeting was also seen by millions all over the world tuned into TBN via television.

It was very meaningful to hear the inspiring words President Ronald Reagan had to say that night on July 5th, 1984.

"Ladies and Gentlemen, nothing could give me greater pleasure than to be able to pay tribute to you, the members of the Full Gospel Business Men's Fellowship. I know your convention must be a cause for joy and celebration. I'm told in the thirty-one years of your existence you have become the largest layman's organization in the world, and I think I know why. Through all those years, you've never looked back, you've always looked up. Up to the one great source of truth and hope, love and beauty, grace and glory, our Father our Creator, our Lord and loving God.

There's a passage from the teachings of Jesus; it's in the book of Mark that I think explains the secret of your success. 'But whoever desires to become great among you, shall be your servant. For even the Son of man did not come to be served but to serve and give his life, a ransom for many.' All this you have done.

For thirty-one years, the Full Gospel Businessmen's Fellowship has been serving America and serving God with all the faith, strength, and courage, that human hearts can bear. It's your commitment and confidence;

your values of faith, family, and freedom that make us know Americans are a good and decent people. And that inspire us to believe America can be a great nation. That's why I said on inauguration day, 'Let us renew our courage and our strength and let us renew our faith and our hope. We have every right to dream heroic dreams, to believe in ourselves. To believe that together with God's help, we can and will resolve the problems which now confront us.'

I believe America is stronger today than we were before; stronger economically, militarily and yes, spiritually too. But what we've succeeded in doing is only a fraction of what needs to be done. How can we rest? How can we be satisfied, knowing that the God who blessed our land, has been expelled from our children's schools? We cannot and we will not.

> *Striving for a spirit of friendship and fellowship among people and nations.*

If enough of us pray together, stand together, and work together than the gates of resistance will fall; and we'll see the day once again when freedom of voluntary vocal prayer has been restored to every classroom in America. And if we can get God and discipline back in our schools, maybe we can get drugs and violence out.

Neither can we rest, nor can the conscience of America be at peace, when the lives of over 4,000 unborn children are being snuffed out every day. Four-thousand children who will never laugh, never sing, never know the joy of human love. Will never strive to heal the sick, feed the poor or make peace among nations. Let us go forth with renewed determination, knowing that no challenge is more important than restoring the right to life. For without that right, no other rights have any meaning.

Within our families and our communities, let us continue reaching out, striving for a spirit of friendship and fellowship among people and nations. Among all who share our lives and our dreams for a better world; and let us remember, that the blessings of liberty we enjoy do not belong to us alone, they are gifts from God. To men and women everywhere we have a duty to support all who struggle for freedom.

We have it within our power, to begin the world all over again. We can be a shining city upon a hill.

Thank you. God Bless you all!"

— President Ronald Reagan
40ᵗʰ President of the United States of America

PRESIDENT FERDINAND MARCOS

It was October 1984 in Asia, when Philippine President Ferdinand Marcos welcomed Grandfather's convention, as they prayed for his country. They heard powerful messages from the great evangelist, T. L. Osborn and Sir Lionel Luckoo, elected four times as the Mayor of Georgetown, Guyana, twice Knighted by Queen Elizabeth ll, and a successful Criminal Attorney.

CONTINUING HIS MISSION,
REGARDLESS OF AN UNEXPECTED OBSTACLE!

In 1984 my Bobby suffered a stroke which left him physically compromised. He now had to walk with a cane. The most upsetting part of it to him was that his speech was impaired. Still, he was determined to continue his mission regardless of this or any other hindrances. So pressing on he continued to spread the love of God.

> "Demos Shakarian impacted several generations worldwide. His vision of reaching men was unstoppable. It was a perfect blend with the great 'Charismatic Movement' which was sweeping the world. I will never forget when he joined us as a guest on our live television program, 'Coast to Coast,' a nightly telecast based in San Francisco and seen throughout the United States for twenty years.
>
> Even though his speech was impaired due to a stroke, his heart still poured out a vision for men, a burden for the world, and a great confidence that the Holy Spirit would finish what Jesus began!"
>
> **— Ronn Haus** • President / TV 42

The World Convention in 1985 was in Melbourne, Australia. Grandfather was excited to announce the special guest speakers, who would share from their heart with the crowd of how God had changed their lives. This included, the incredible evangelist Reinhard Bonnke, Jack Hayford who is Chancellor of The Kings University, Lee Buck who left his position as Senior Vice President of New York's Life marketing to enter full-time ministry, Bill Subritzky a senior partner of a law firm in New Zealand and Director of one of his nation's largest home-building companies.

In 1986 Congressman Bill Nelson, who was Chairman of the House Sub-Committee on Space, shared with Grandfather's organization. He trained with Christa McAuliffe, a teacher who became the first American civilian selected to go into space, and was slated for Nasa's *Columbia* flight. This was the last successful flight before the disastrous *Challenger* flight, where Christa was tragically killed. He explained the most memorable part of the *Columbia* voyage. "The stars were so brilliant, I could see forever. I was constantly reminded of Psalm 19:1: 'The Heavens declare the glory of the Lord, and the skies proclaim the work of His hands.'"

Then in April 1986, John DeLorean, an executive at General Motors, founder of DeLorean Motor Company, and designer of the sports car featured in the film *Back to the Future*; also shared his journey to finding Christ.

Later that year, the World Convention was held in Orlando, Florida at the grand *Marriott's Orlando World Center*. Speaking powerful messages were James Robison, former Kentucky Governor Julian Carroll, "Big" John Hall, Mike Murdock and Charles Fay, the Vice President of A.G. Edwards Company.

The Military Breakfast was excited to hear special guest speakers, General Charles Duke and General Fred Mahaffey.

THE COVER OF A MAGAZINE!

In June 1986 my grandfather was honored when *Charisma Magazine* put him on the cover of their magazine stating:

> "We salute Demos Shakarian who has made an invaluable contribution to the development of the Pentecostal movement worldwide.
>
> Ponder this, an international army of tens of thousands influential businessmen poised to deliver the world from suffering. Your first response to his life story

may be the epitome of satire or *a Hollywood script,* but certainly not the substance of history.

That is unless you're among the millions who have been within the visionary reach of Demos Shakarian and the legacy of his tireless life.

The personal saga of Demos' spiritual pilgrimage is an intricately woven tapestry of ancestral roots, prophetic visions, timely miracles, unwavering faith, and an obsession with hard work. But it has always been his just-plain-folks demeanor which makes for a surprising first impression.

You expect an intimidating figure with the charisma and leadership traits commensurate for a man of his station in life. You instead meet a man who disarms you with a winsome spirit and you-have-my-undivided-attention look in his eye."

It was very humbling for Grandfather to receive such worldwide attention for following what he believed; he was put on this earth to do. He was merely fulfilling his purpose!

A PRISON OUTREACH

Around 1987, members of my grandfather's organization created a large prison ministry called "Set Free." This outreach visited inmates sharing the love of God. There were 31 chapters who became actively involved in the program.

In February 1991, Ben Burtt shared how after asking God into his heart, he asked the Lord to run his life. He was overflowing with gratitude as he won an Academy Award. He had worked on *Star Wars, Indiana Jones and the Last Crusade,*

Raiders of the Lost Ark, and *E.T., The Extra-Terrestrial*.

Dr. Ben Carson who was raised in Detroit by a single parent and became a successful Neurosurgeon shared his

> "A man who disarms you with a winsome spirit and you-have-my-undivided-attention look in his eye."

incredible story. He told, "How God gave a dream to a discouraged ghetto kid who wanted to become a doctor." Years later, he would become the U.S. Secretary of Housing and Urban Development.

In 1987, a Regional Convention was held in Washington D.C., at the *Omni Sheraton Hotel*. Speakers included Marilyn Hickey and Charles and Frances Hunter. That year Gene Ellerbee, the manager of sales at Procter & Gamble shared about his complete faith in God.

Also in 1987, Martin Angelo, Jr who worked with ex-Beatle John Lennon, Jimi Hendrix, Janis Joplin and Jethro Tull, shared with my grandfather's organization; about his journey which led him to ask Jesus into his life.

Then in October, Jeff Fenholt shared how finding Christ changed his life. He had previously played the original Jesus in "Jesus Christ Superstar" and sang lead for *Black Sabbath*. With his life transformed by the power of God, he was now speaking at many of Grandfather's meetings!

A CHRISTMAS TO REMEMBER

There are so many times I thought I knew my grandfather well but all through my life, he continued to amaze me at the most unexpected times.

The Christmas of 1992, my Bobby was 79 years old. He was sentimental about spending Christmas Eve together with all of the family, which was our custom. Those nights were always filled with wonderful traditions, including singing Christmas songs.

This Christmas Eve felt especially exciting. My daughter, Rachel, was three-years-old and now understood the meaning of gift giving! The family would gather at my grandparents' home for our Christmas celebration. Every year my grandmother would invite someone who would be alone that year, to join our family celebration. This Christmas Eve was no exception.

With the decline of my grandparent's health, there was a big change that year. They were no longer physically able to host the celebration at their home. When I think back on all the Christmas' with my grandparents, the times I remember is when our Christmas Eve celebration was still held in their home in Downey, California.

CHRISTMAS EVE NIGHT

These were the traditions of the evening which started at my grandparent's home and played out in the same order every year.

Everyone would excitedly gather at my grandparent's large Spanish style two-story home, which was formerly my great-grandfather Isaacs'. The women would disappear into the kitchen putting the last minute touches on the Christmas dinner, and the men sat close to the family Christmas Tree talking about "who knows what."

I enjoyed most hearing my three-year-old calling it Over-Sea's Candy!

I attribute my love for *See's Candy* to my grandparents, because every Christmas there would be two candy dishes full of *See's Candy* in the living room. One candy dish was placed on the piano and the other one on a table close to the organ. Though it is still my favorite chocolate, what I enjoyed most was hearing my three-year-old calling it, *Over-Sea's Candy*! A clue that she had been raised in a family who traveled the world!

Amused my Uncle Steve asked me, "Why are you standing by the door?" While enjoying my piece of choco-late-mocha I answered him, "I'm waiting for the carolers to come and serenade us. You know, they always come around this time." The minute I finished saying that I heard them knock on the door.

I loved when the carolers came as they would be dressed in outfits which looked like they were right out of the 1800's. We offered them refreshments for their caroling. When they left dinner was served. I could hardly wait because our Christmas Eve meal was my favorite.

There was plenty of string cheese, flatbread and a relish dish full of celery, olives, pickles, and radishes on the table. With the size of our family, there was an adult's table in the dining room and the children's table in the breakfast room. I never did graduate to the adult table. All the grandchildren continued calling it the kids' table, no matter how old we were. It was always fun joking to see who would be the first to be moved to eat with the adults.

The meal included turkey and stuffing, green beans with sautéed tomatoes, and yams with brown sugar and melted marshmallows. Also served was jello with pineapples and sliced strawberries with sour crème on top, and the wedding pilaf. There were plenty of pies and shaka-loof for dessert!

*He was dressed
and ready to party
for the Lord –
Demos style!*

My favorite dish was the wedding pilaf, served with raisins, dates, and slivered almonds, which had been sautéed together in butter and placed on top of the pilaf. This was a special treat for Christmas, and it was always a special treat for me.

After dinner, we all gathered around the Christmas Tree which was now full of presents. This is when everyone's musical talents would come out. Or lack thereof! My Aunt Geri who is incredibly gifted musically always played the piano, with my grandmother playing the organ. Everyone else held bells strung together with Christmas ribbon and small musical instruments, anything that would add to the joyous occasion.

By now the little kids would be rushing the singing along, anxious to get to the gift-opening part of the evening. But there was still one more important event which had to take place first. This was the most important part of the evening.

After we sung several songs, which would include *Holy Night* and *The Twelve Days of Christmas*, it was time for my grandfather to tell the Christmas Story! He sat in a big chair placed so everyone could see him. Holding his Bible, he read stories of Jesus, giving his personal commentary along the way. Then he prayed as we gave thanks for the true reason we are celebrating this day, Jesus' birth! Wow, how I would love to hear him tell the story and pray one more time, as he thanked God for all the blessings He had given us that year. Then it was time to open presents. My Bobby always made it a memorable Christmas Eve!

CHRISTMAS DAY

That year I was blessed to help organize an event inspired by Joe Ferlauto, called *Christmas Cheer*. It involved providing a full Christmas lunch for underprivileged families in Los Angeles County. This was to be held on Christmas Day 1992, in a large gymnasium in the park, completely transformed with beautiful Christmas decorations.

Holding his Bible he would read stories of Jesus giving his personal commentary along the way.

A full turkey dinner would be served to hundreds of families who would not ordinarily be able to celebrate Christmas. This included presents for all of the kids, from babies to teenagers.

I knew one thing for sure; we had to open the event in prayer. I thought who better to say the prayer than my Bobby, Demos. I wasn't sure if he would be up to it physically because I knew we would have our large Armenian Christmas Eve the night before. I was concerned he might grow tired.

He spent his last Christmas like always, blessing others!

When I finally nonchalantly mentioned it to him, his response is something I will never forget. He could not have been more enthusiastic. Without hesitation, he said, "I can't think of anything I would rather do on Christmas Day! What time should I be there?"

Christmas morning Bobby was the first to arrive even before the doors were unlocked. He was dressed and ready to party for the Lord – Demos style! No one was more excited to be there than my Bobby. Not even the hundreds of children and their families who showed up. My Bobby with a cane in hand was helped up on the stage to the microphone. After speaking for a few minutes, Grandfather said an anointed prayer as he prayed a blessing over everyone. It was a beautiful moment etched in my heart forever!

Little did I know this would be his last Christmas here on earth. True to his nature he spent his last Christmas like always . . . serving others!

HIS LAST INTERNATIONAL CONVENTION

By the spring of 1993, the summer was quickly approaching as I prepared to attend the 40th International Convention of my grandfather's organization, which was held every year in July. It was always an enjoyable time as I expected to see many of my family members in attendance.

It was a wonderful celebration for his 80th birthday.

My daughter, Rachel was about to turn four-years-old and excited to be with *her Bobby*, my dad Richard and *her Great-Bobby*, my grandfather Demos. The convention was held in Boston, Massachusetts and we couldn't wait to get there.

While I was packing for our trip, I explained to my daughter her Great-Bobby's 80th Birthday was coming up later that month. She was so excited. To my young daughter, birthdays meant one thing . . . Cake!

Arriving at the hotel in Boston, I found out because of conflicting schedules many of the family members were not able to make it that year. Looking back on it, this year was very unusual as I was the only grandchild, and my daughter, Rachel, was the only great-grandchild of my grandparents, who would be attending. To this day, I am so grateful my daughter and I were able to be there. Little did anyone know this would be my Bobby's last days.

John Hagee, the Pastor of Cornerstone Church in San Antonio, Texas and many others, gave incredible messages.

The highlight happened in one of the evening meetings when some of the International Representatives brought out a huge cake, and everyone sang *Happy Birthday* to my grandfather. Dozens of children of all ages joyfully walked as in a festive parade. They were carrying red, white and blue balloons, dressed in their Sunday best. It was a wonderful celebration for his 80th birthday, and I was thrilled to see him recognized in this way. It was well deserved for a man who had given so much to others.

PRESIDENT BILL CLINTON

As beautiful words and blessings were spoken, it was marvelous to hear even the current President of the United States; President Bill Clinton had sent my grandfather a birthday greeting that night on July 3, 1993.

"Congratulations and best wishes! You have reached an important milestone in your life, and I join with you in that celebration!"

— President Bill Clinton
42nd President of the United States of America

CHAPTER TWENTY

14 Days of Cherished Memories

Grandfather's health was beginning to decline and I was cherishing every moment I had left with him. I began to fully realize who my grandfather was and who I wanted to become.

The year was around 1984 and I was twenty-something. My grandmother was recovering from surgery and asked me to help her for two weeks. While helping my grandmother through the day, I continued to be drawn to my Bobby. As he would tell me stories of his yesterday, I could see the passion he had for humanity. He spoke about the injustice and the poor throughout the world. Sitting with him at night before falling asleep, I could feel his passion slowly rising in me. I felt God was igniting compassion in me to somehow be a part in changing the world.

I never thought I would only have my grandfather, my mentor, for just a few years more.

PRIVATE MOMENTS

My grandparents, still living in Downey had turned the front room off the entry into a den. This was where my grandfather would read and often be found on his knees talking with the Lord. Though, he spent time with God everywhere

> *My grandfather would often be found on his knees talking with the Lord.*

he went.

My Bobby's front room was so cozy. It had two small couches, a coffee table full of newspapers and a small television. I felt surrounded by love whenever I entered that room. Curled up on one of the couches, I listened to more of their adventures as my grandparents shared numerous old photos with me. The floors of the home were covered in dark Spanish tiles, and I kept curling my toes onto the warm couch to keep them off the cold floor.

I remember thinking, *this might be the last time I hear these stories directly from them.* I wanted everything to be etched upon my heart. Especially their laughter which was memorable. Grandfather also had such a great sense of humor.

Though the stories were not just adventures anymore to me, I realized that Kara Kala was not a town from *Fiddler on the Roof.* These were stories about my family members making critical decisions that would affect our family for generations to come.

Somehow being with my grandparents felt different this time, perhaps because neither of us was rushing off someplace, or because I was old enough to understand the gravity of what they were sharing with me. Either way, this time was a gift of memories wrapped in love which I will always cherish.

Life often hands us these special moments, and if we are

> *This time was a gift of memories wrapped in love which I will always cherish.*

present enough to accept them, we capture something which will never come our way again. This is what these fourteen memorable days with my grandfather and my grandmother were to me.

Initially, I viewed this time as helping my grandmother recover from surgery, but I was wrong. My efforts to help my grandparents

But my next-to-him seat in his den . . . was my favorite!

during the days I stayed with them turned into a major blessing in my life, an everlasting treasure. I received much more during those two weeks than I gave them.

I picture in my mind the European rugs my grandparents had throughout the house and the beautiful decorations from their travels all over the world. My grandmother loved deep red and blue, and these accent colors flowed from room to room. As a little girl, their home seemed almost magical because I felt drawn there. Now I know what I sensed was the strong presence of the Holy Spirit.

MY NEXT-TO-HIM SEAT

Looking back on my innocent childhood years when my grandfather was just my Bobby; I realize now that on more than one occasion I had a privileged perspective. I had a front-row seat which pointed straight to the future of my grandfather, as the gentle-man who would eventually lead millions of people closer to the Holy Spirit.

I had a front-row seat at many of the conventions. I had a front-row seat at his favorite coffee shop, Foxy's Restaurant, and while socializing with him at the neighborhood car wash.

I had a front-row seat while observing him in his office at his International Headquarters.

But my next-to-him seat in his den . . . was my favorite!

GOLD MEDAL MEMORIES

By this time my grandfather had suffered a stroke. He was physically unable to take care of my grandmother after her surgery. During this time he slept in another room. In case she needed anything I slept with her in their huge California King bed, my grandmother on one side and I on the other. As we talked, I remember being so warm in their cozy bed, running my hand over the delicate baby-blue lace coverlet, which covered the sheets.

The athletes were making lifetime memories of their own, while I was hearing mine!

We had the Winter Olympics turned on the television as it was something we both enjoyed watching. I listened to Momie as if it was the first time she was sharing her memories with me. We turned the sound down low on the television, occasionally glancing over to see who had won a Gold Medal.

I would always feel as if I were a little taller, quite a bit thinner, and much smarter!

My grandmother and I sat on her bed, while the snow skiers raced down the hill in the background. The athletes were making lifetime memories of their own, while I was hearing mine!

In the mornings I would make my way to Orange County, which was about a 45-minute drive to my Real Estate office. At day's end, I couldn't wait to drive back to my grandparents' home.

Grandfather seemed very pleased that I was in real estate. Every time he would introduce me as a real estate agent, it appeared to me that he was very proud of my accomplishments.

In actuality, my Bobby was proud of everything I did. Well, almost everything! After spending time with him, I would always feel as if I were a little taller, quite a bit thinner, and much smarter! I felt invincible. He found the best qualities deep inside me, and he knew how to bring them to the surface.

A different focus toward the future as if the Lord had given me a new lens.

Grandfather encouraged me to believe, I could do anything God put on my heart to do. He encouraged me to not limit myself, as God always see's more in us than we usually see in ourselves. And I believe, my Bobby was seeing more in me.

He called out the gifts within me saying, *I had a heart for humanity just like he did. Seeing injustices and desiring to right the wrongs in the world.*

I didn't realize how he had watched me on many occasions, helping those less fortunate. My negotiating skills, which had been sharpened by my years of selling real estate was also something he related to. Telling me *how important it would be in my future.*

When my 14 days with my grandparents came to an end, I knew I would never again have an opportunity quite like I had with them. Leaving their home on the last day of my visit, I realized I now had a different focus toward the future, as if I had been given a new lens. No longer seeing what was behind me, but looking to what was ahead.

I looked to my destiny that day selling real estate, and soon I would be preparing for the wedding of my dreams. The Lord had blessed my work as a Real Estate agent, becoming one of the top agents where I worked. I was also about to walk down the aisle. I was getting married! Though I had no idea those fourteen days with my grandparents started a journey, which eventually would lead me to write this book.

A GAME CHANGER!

My Bobby went to heaven just two weeks after the last International Convention in Boston. I can only imagine the glorious welcome my grandfather experienced. I picture it as trumpets blaring with his parents Isaac and Zarouhi, and his baby daughter Caroline among the first to greet him. With *his* beloved grandfather, Demos who he was named after but he had never met, standing not far behind. Although as I envision it, nothing thrilled him more than hearing those seven words he had so longed to hear from his Heavenly Father, "Well done my good and faithful servant!"

It is no wonder he chose the sign 'His Banner Over Us Is Love' to have up during his meetings.

Many who had gone to visit him at the hospital had sensed angels filling the hallways and surrounding the hospital. It appeared as though they were getting ready to welcome home this General of Faith. Oral Roberts, visiting my grandfather said, "The angels are preparing the way because a Patriarch and a Prophet is about to go home!"

While on this earth my grandfather was a "Game Changer!" This term is often used in sporting events, but I believe it applies to Grandfather. He put together a model of a business organization, which influenced people around the world for Christ and launched numerous ministries. All while keeping his integrity and standing up for what he believed was the right thing to do. He stepped out in his kind and loving way, but with "Bull-Dog Faith." He continued his purpose, through all the obstacles. Yes, he was truly a man of honor.

Through incredibly challenging times in my life, I have found God has also shown me what I needed to take another step. Receiving many prophetic words has given me con-

He stepped out in his kind and loving way, but with "Bull-Dog Faith."

firmation and renewed my strength to also press on. They have encouraged me to continue moving forward, stepping into God's purpose and plan for my life. As this one did, prophesied to me in a church service on August 2, 2015.

"Your book *The Shakarian Legacy*, about your grandfather is not just a call to remembrance. It is important people do not forget your grandfather and all the good things which he brought forth. He brought businessmen together and united them. He brought pastors together of different associations. He did something at a time when it was difficult to bring everyone together. He united the businessmen, and the Lord is using you to keep the vision ... Alive!

It's not going to just be about remembering him and what this great man did, but God is going to use it to reunite, reunite the fire of some things. Where people have had no unity, there is going to be a unity that is going to begin to come into the body of Christ, and into the Church. And the Lord is going to use you to be a part of it. Thus saith the Lord!

I see what is about to happen is going to reach into some other countries. You're going to be called on by some people out of other countries to come, and a vision of some things is going to begin in other places. It's all going to happen out of what God is using you right now to bring forth. Thus saith the Lord!"

— Howard Richardson • Prophet, Pastor / Gates of Glory

MY GRANDFATHER, MY BOBBY REMEMBERED

July 23, 1993, was a sad day for millions of people touched by my grandfather's life. My Bobby was eighty-years-old when he passed away. In fact, it was two days after his 80th birthday. Looking back, I wish he had asked for many more years.

After Grandfather's passing, my father, Richard Shakarian, was then appointed the *Lifetime International President.*

His memorial service was led by his good friend Oral Roberts. In attendance were well over one-thousand people who came to honor my Bobby, Demos Shakarian. Oral Roberts spoke lovingly of my grandfather and Great-grandfather, Isaac. Saying:

> "Their names were everywhere, becoming leaders in their community and leaders in the Christian world. When from as far back as 1951, I started hearing about this great family on the West Coast.
>
> Oral Roberts Ministry was planning on holding meetings which were to be held in Oakland, California, but we were having difficulty in obtaining use of the location which was selected. Just when we thought the meetings might have to be canceled, it was suggested we call and see if the Shakarians' in California could help get the permission we needed. We contacted Lee Braxton and asked if he could assist in reaching Demos Shakarian. It was by the Shakarian's influence the city opened a choice spot. This continued in Los Angeles and San Francisco.
>
> He was the sweetest-spirited man I have ever known, and his name was Demos Shakarian. It is no wonder he chose the sign 'His Banner Over Us Is Love' to have up during his meetings. In my opinion, Demos

was the greatest layman in the world, winning more souls for Christ than any other I know of. He brought Christ salvation using hotels, factories, offices, and headquarters of governments to draw the masses.

I remember when his organization was only a seed in the mind of one man, Demos Shakarian. I told him, 'Demos, you must do it!' Later Demos and I talked with Isaac about the ramifications of Demos being away from the dairy business. Isaac said, 'Demos you go, and I'll take care of the business."

He went on to share how my grandfather had faithfully been on the Oral Roberts University Evangelistic Association Board for thirty years. Both of my grandparents never missed a meeting. Grandfather was also elected Vice-Chairman of the Board for some time, so Oral explained: "If something had happened to me, Demos would have been the Chairman."

Paul Crouch of Trinity Broadcasting Network shared, "This is a celebration of a great soldier's life. What an abundant entrance this dear man must have just made in Heaven. One of the things I loved most about Demos was he was always friendly. There was a smile on his face. You always felt you could sit down and share the deepest problems of your life with him. He was a great inspiration to Jan and me." He also praised my grandfather's negotiating skills while always a consummate businessman.

Paul also shared how some of his leading advisors told him; he could not show the power of the Holy Spirit on television. My grandfather who was on the Board of TBN when it first began, disagreed completely. Grandfather explained, "The world needs to see God's supernatural power, or the world will show them theirs."

> *"I want to say
> he loved every one of you.
> He had a great heart
> for humanity."*

Many, many others also contributed their thoughts about my grandfather. Such as Kwabena Darko from Africa who said, "Demos would advise you. He would encourage you, and he would pray for you." Bernie Gray from the South Pacific expressed his feelings, "Demos is a man in whom I have seen the love of Jesus oozing out, and it spills out all over. I felt like I needed to salute this warrior of God."

Pastor Harding Mushegan shared with the overflowing crowd, "The words I'm about to say is about a man who walked with God and loved people! Demos Shakarian was a Dairyman and a Real Estate Developer. With his father, Isaac, they built the largest independently owned dairy in the world, owning 5,000 milking cows. He was a pillar of the community.

Demos was appointed by two Governors, Pat Brown and Ronald Reagan, to the State of California Agricultural Board. He also helped to build Downey Hospital. Through his organization he changed the lives of men and women throughout the world, touching over 120 countries!"

Grandfather was grateful to have celebrated a number of wonderful milestones in his life.

In 1993, Grandfather saw his worldwide organization exceed their *40th Anniversary*.

He had also seen the *50th Anniversary* of his dairy farm, becoming the largest independently owned in the world.

My grandparents were two weeks away from celebrating their *60th Wedding Anniversary*.

Grandfather had celebrated his *80th Birthday*!

Beautiful messages poured in from around the world including former President Jimmy Carter. At the gravesite, one-hundred-sixty white doves were released. They circled the crowd before flying away.

CELEBRATING DEMOS SHAKARIAN'S LIFE

When the memorial service was over and true to tradition, a feast immediately followed. The guests dined at a sit-down dinner, as speeches and fun stories about Grandfather were retold. It was wonderful to see Grandfather honored in such a remarkable way. But without a doubt, what he would have been the most pleased with, was the stories of the lives which were

The legacy he left is a cornerstone, to continue on in this current generation.

changed when they first became acquainted with their Lord and Savior, at one of Grandfather's meetings. It was wonderful to hear how the power of God healed businesses and families after attending his meeting somewhere around the world. What a marvelous time of celebrating my Bobby's life and his legacy.

My Aunt Geri spoke about what a gentle spirit her father had while she was growing up. My grandmother said it perfectly while addressing the crowd, "I want to say he loved every one of you. He had a great heart for humanity. His desire was to see the world saved. He wanted to put his arms around everyone he met and love them unto the Lord."

Momie choked up as she spoke softly, holding back tears. She knew Grandfather was smiling down at her. As the memories of all they had

His example has inspired many, but none more than me, his granddaughter.

been through, came flooding through her mind. She knew he was with his Heavenly Father. That was all she needed to know. After a life-long journey which had become quite an adventure, he was at last with his Lord and Savior.

It was three years later on June 15, 1996, that Grandmother Rose, Momie, went to be with The Lord joining my grandfather. Oral Roberts would sometimes call her *Rose of Sharon*. She was also lovingly honored for her steadfastness in following the voice of the Lord and encouraging my grandfather to step out in faith. She played a significant role in everything coming to pass!

That same year in 1996, the International Headquarters of my grandfather's organization in Costa Mesa, California was sold to Trinity Broadcasting Network. TBN would sell it in 2017.

FINDING YOUR PURPOSE

What I learned from my Bobby is, it does not matter where you are starting from, it only matters what God has spoken in your heart. Keep your eyes set on your vision, your dream, and on God. Soon . . . you will be walking into your Destiny!

> *It is from a very different perspective, and through completely different lenses.*

As I consider now who my grandfather was, I understand his legacy was bringing people together in love to fulfill God's purpose in their lives. He encouraged others to find their unique talent and special purpose and pursue it. He knew finding that particular ability and using it would be where we will find the most fulfillment in our life. He always saw the best in people even when they didn't see it in themselves and introduced thousands to the power of the Holy Spirit.

My grandfather's goal was to cover the world with the love of God, person by person, and city by city. The legacy he left is a cornerstone to continue in this current generation.

Truly my Bobby has left big shoes to fill indeed. His example has inspired many but none more than me, his granddaughter. He has been my true inspiration!

> Through it all,
> He has been gently
> leading me through my
> journey, to my legacy,
> and my destiny.

I thank God for that foundation because God has extended this vision in me to include men, women, and all humanity. A seed was placed in me as I realized that he allowed Aimee Semple McPherson and Kathryn Kuhlman to speak from his platform, when it was practically unheard of. I thought; *Yes, I want to help and encourage women to rise.*

Encouraging words helped me to view the obstacles and hurdles I've gone through in a different light. I was amazed, just like my grandfather, when he received very similar words from God through Milton the painter and a confirming word from the pastor. Though he received the words into his heart and knew they were from God, he had no idea how the words would come to pass.

Similarly, I received the prophecy by Prophet Richardson previously written and confirmed on multiple occasions over the last number of years, by many of God's Prophets. Like the following prophecy, given to me on March 29, 2017.

"Through *The Shakarian Legacy*, Cynthia Sharkarian is bringing a new insight and heartfelt understanding to the legacy of her family. She, like her grandfather has a heart for humanity, healing the broken hearted and bringing justice to the abused through her organization, "The Demos Shakarian Foundation" which is her passion.

Cynthia, by meeting many Diplomats, Presidents and Heads of State you will reach nations and countries. You are a visionary, a humanitarian and a philanthropist. What you are Cynthia Shakarian, is one of God's own Ambassadors for humanity."

— **Al G. Forniss** • Apostle, Doctor, Prophet / Al Forniss Ministries

I just thank God for these words of encouragement. And like my grandfather I will wait and see how, and when, the Lord will bring these words to pass.

LOOKING TO THE FUTURE

At the time I started writing this book my life held some challenges I had never faced before. My grandparents also faced unexpected obstacles on their journey, and they always overcame them by their faith in God and their message of love. Because of their example, I have learned to surrender to His leading. Sometimes I can hear them in my heart encouraging me not to give up!

Remembering everything my grandfather and his father had been through in their lives, I can now relate to their experiences in ways I never thought, or ever imagined, I could. God has been revealing His truth to me as I write about my grandfather's pilgrimage. Through it all, He has been gently leading me through my journey, to my legacy, and my destiny.

It is my heart's desire, this book will help to lead you to the fulfillment of your vision and purpose as well. For you to press on and enlarge the dreams in your heart, and complete your destiny which only you can fulfill.

What were you born to do? If you are unsure, pray and start moving putting one foot in front of the other towards what is in your heart. You will be surprised with each step, more will be revealed. Soon you will be able to see your destiny unfold before your eyes as you continue taking steps forward, just as my grandfather did.

As a young adult, spending those precious 14 days with my grandparents, I knew nothing about the journey my life was about to take. For the most part, my life had followed the theme song of my favorite childhood movie; Cinderella. The song is, "A Dream Is A Wish Your Heart Makes," and I thought all my dreams were about to come true. Well – that was my plan anyway.

Up to that point, I had never experienced the kind of devastating heartbreak I had only heard about. Never realizing the twists and turns my life would take, bringing me to this point in my journey.

The time I spent with my grandparents was exciting and a highlight of my life. Though I am now looking forward to my future, from a very different perspective, and through a completely different lens. As I feel a calling to continue sharing Grandfather's legacy of uniting all humanity with the love of God.

Thank you for being with me on this adventure and the heritage and legacy which God gave us all. You see, I am still on my journey and I know there are more steps to be taken, more hills to climb, and I know, more stories to be told.

Like a gymnast running towards the springboard to leap over the vault, I feel this book is my springboard into my future and the visions that my Bobby helped me to see. Jump with me, see you there!

With Deep Gratitude

"Thank you" to everyone who was part of my grandfather's vision, dream, and destiny. Plus those who helped in seeing my dream for this book, become a reality. Grandfather was truly honored by your participation and loved you all, just as I do!

Those named below were either a part of my grandfather's organization or contributed in some way to the fulfillment of his vision. The list includes people from all walks of life.

To those not individually named, my love and appreciation go out to you as well! I sincerely Thank You!

Nancy Alcorn • President / Mercy Ministries

Blaine Amburgy • Blaine Development Corporation

Martin Angelo, Jr. • Worked with Jimmy Hendricks, John Lennon, Janis Joplin, Jethro Tull

Steve Archer • Grammy Award Winning Singer / Member of "The Archers"

Miner Arganbright • Masonry Contractor

Humberto Arguello • Exc. International Treasurer, Nicaragua, under Dad's Presidency

Thomas Ashcraft • Baking company executive / On Grandfather's Executive Committee

Jim Bakker • Pastor / Host, The Jim Bakker Show

Eddy Reyes Baldizon • International Director, Nicaragua, under my dad's Presidency

Jerry and Sandi Barnard • Pastors / The Horizon Church

Tommy Barnett • Founder Los Angeles Dream Center & Phoenix Dream Center

John Barton • Chairman Board of International Directors for Grandfather's organization

Father Dennis Bennett • A Spirit-filled Episcopalian Priest

Mike Bergita • Notre Dame University

Bruno Berthon • Co-Chair Global Advisory Council, International Field of Energy; France

Robert Birdsong • "Mr. Universe"

Dale Black • TWA Pilot

Walter Bloch • Television Script Writer for Hawaii Five-O and Bonanza

Walter Block • Successful Businessman, Director for my grandfather's organization

John Blue • Boston Bruins Goalie

Sylvester Blue • Powerful Singer

Major Gary Bluemink • United States Army Surgeon at Walter Reed Hospital

William Bond • U.S. Navy / Received a Medal of Honor / Construction Business

Reinhard Bonnke • Evangelist / Christ For All Nations

Corrie Ten Boom • Imprisoned for aiding Jewish victims, saving approximately 800 lives

Pat Boone • Singer, Actor, Entertainer, Hollywood Walk of Fame

Colonel Heath Bottomly • Graduated from West Point / Decorated Fighter Pilot

Kermit Bradford • Attorney in Georgia / Army Intelligence Officer

William Branham • Influential American Minister / Impacted the Charismatic Movement

Lee Braxton • Chairman of the Board First National Bank, Grandfather's Executive Committee

Harold Bredesen • Spirit-filled Dutch Reformed Church Pastor

Billye Brim • Billye Brim Ministries / Prayer Mountain in the Ozarks

Pierce Brooks • Founder of the National Banker's Life Insurance Company

Lee Buck • New York Life Insurance

Jim Buick • President / Buck Knives, Inc.

Ray and his son Don Bullard • Of Bullard and Sons Construction

Allan and Anoosh Bullock • Missionary Evangelists

Ben Burtt • Winner of Four Academy Awards / Won Sound-Effects for Star Wars / Won Sound-Editing for "Indiana Jones and the Last Crusade" / Worked on "Raiders of the Lost Ark" / "Invasion of the Body Snatchers" / "E.T., the Extra-Terrestrial"

Sir Milo Butler • Appointed as the first Bahamian Governor-General

Bruno Caamano • Founder / Almavision Network

Daniel Caamano • President / AtlasBanc Holdings Corporation

Charles Capps • An incredible Word of Faith Christian teacher

Charles Carney • Braniff Airline Pilot

Lieutenant Colonel Merlin Carothers • U.S. Army, 82nd Airborne Demolition Expert / Guard for Dwight D. Eisenhower / Master Parachutist, Civil Air Patrol Pilot

Charlie Carpenter • Builder in Pasadena, California

Barbara Kardashian Carr • My grandfather's second cousin

Governor Julian Carroll • Former Kentucky Governor

Dr. Ben Carson • Neurosurgeon / U.S. Secretary of Housing & Urban Development

President Jimmy Carter • 39th President of the United States

Johnny Cash • Singer, Songwriter, Guitarist / One of the most influential musicians

Fidel Castro • President of Cuba

Morris Cerullo • Founder / Morris Cerullo World Evangelism

Roberto Chihan • CBN TV / International Director under Dad's Presidency; Paraguay

Mark Chironna • Pastor / Church on the Living Edge

Dr. David Yonggi Cho • Founder / Yoido Full Gospel Church, South Korea

Enoch Christofferson • Mayor of Turlock, California / an independent Turkey grower

Kim Clement • Founder, Prophet / Kim Clement Center

President Bill Clinton • 42nd President of the United States: July 3, 1993

Jack Coe • Evangelist, Faith Leader

Honorable Eve Cohen • Administrative Law Judge

Pete Congelliere • Businessman / Served in my grandfather's organization

Bayless Conley • Pastor / Cottonwood Church

Francisco Contreras, M.D. • Chairman / Oasis of Hope Hospital

Garth Coonce • TCT Network / Int'l Director, under my dad's Presidency; USA

Adolph Coors • Coors Brewery

A W. Copeland • Father of Kenneth Copeland

Kenneth and Gloria Copeland • Founders / Kenneth Copeland Ministries

Andrae Crouch • Pastor, Gospel Singer, Songwriter, Producer / Conducted the choirs on Michael Jackson's "Man in the Mirror." Received seven Grammy Awards, induction into the Gospel Music Hall of Fame, and a star on the Hollywood Walk of Fame

Paul and Jan Crouch • Founders / Trinity Broadcasting Network

Nicky Cruz • Subject of the movie The Cross and the Switchblade

R. L. Culpepper • Prayed for the youth outside the Shrine Auditorium

Loren Cunningham • Founder / YWAM

Richard J. Daley • Mayor of Chicago, Illinois

Kwabena Darko • International Director under my grandfather and Dad's Presidency; Held "Leadership Seminars" in 40 countries; Chief Officer / Darko Farms & Co. LTD; Ghana

John DeLorean • Widely known for his work at General Motors / Founder of the DeLorean Motor Company / Designed the sports car featured in the 1985 film Back to the Future

Arlene Vikse Del Rio • Pastor / Abounding Grace Ministries

Gratien De Souza • International Director, Togo, under my dad's Presidency; Alfaco Ltd.

Paul Dhinakaran, Ph.D. • President / Jesus Calls International, India

Earl Draper • Businessman / Fresno, California

Dave Dravecky • Baseball's San Francisco Giants / San Diego Padres

Phil Driscoll • Trumpeter, Singer, Composer, Producer / Won a Grammy Award / Won three Dove Awards and the 1999 Christian Country Music Association Award

Brigadier General Charles Duke • Former Navy Officer / Air Force Test Pilot / Astronaut

Jesse Duplantis • Founder / Jesse Duplantis Ministries

David du Plessis • Spread the Holy Spirit to churches worldwide; South Africa

President Francois Duvalier • President of Haiti

Jack Eckerd • Eckerd's Drug Store Chain

Elf Ekman • Pastor and the Founder of Livets Ord (Word of Life) organization in Sweden

Gene Ellerby • Worldwide Manager of Sales for Procter & Gamble

Al Enderle • Businessman, Irvine, California

Howard Ervin • Pastor / Emmanuel Baptist Church, Atlantic Highlands, N.J.

Neil Eskelin • Member of the International Youth Board for Grandfather's organization

Ekere Essien • International Director, Nigeria, under my dad's Presidency

Sundry Essien • International Director, Nigeria, under my dad's Presidency

Gideon Esurua • International Director, Nigeria, under my dad's Presidency

Charles Fay • Vice President of A.G. Edwards Company

Jeff Fenholt • Played "Jesus" in the original Jesus Christ Superstar / Cover of Time Magazine / Lead vocalist for Black Sabbath

Paul B. Fischer • Attorney specializing in Corporate Organizations

Chuck and Mary Ann Flynn • Engineer on the DC-10 at McDonnell Douglas / Prophets

Clifford C. "C.C." Ford • Banker and Developer

Al G. Forniss • Apostle / Al Forniss Ministries

Ruben Fuentes • Sergeant with the Austin, Texas Police Force

George Gardner • New York Businessman

Velmer Gardner • Evangelist

Mel Gibson • Starred in Braveheart, Won Golden Globe Award & Academy Award for Best Picture / Produced, The Passion of the Christ / Directed, Hacksaw Ridge

Wayne Gillie • Inspector with General Motors, Canada

John Gimenez • Organized Washington for Jesus where my grandfather spoke

Kelso Glover • Evangelist

Colonel Henry Godman • United States Army

Dr. Henry Gore • Math Professor at Morehouse College

J. Peter Grace • Leader of an industrial firm / a B.A. from Yale University / Selected by President Reagan to head President's Private Sector Survey on Cost Control

Rev Billy Graham • The Billy Graham Crusades / One of the most influential Christian leaders

Hugh S. Graham • Vice-President of the Cal-U-Nite Corporation

Tommy Green • Owned an NBA Store

Roosevelt (Rosey) Grier • All-Pro New York Giants / Played five World Championship Games / Helped apprehend gunman who assassinated Robert F. Kennedy

John Hagee • Senior Pastor, Cornerstone Church / Founder, Christians United for Israel

Kenneth E. Hagin, Jr • Rhema Ministries / Kenneth Hagin Ministries

Kenneth W. Hagin, Sr • Founder / Kenneth Hagin Ministries

General Ralph Haines • Four Star Commanding General, U.S. Continental Army Command

"Big" John Hall • Musical Gospel Artist

Wes Hall • West Indies Cricket Hall of Fame / Barbados Senate, House of Assembly

Major Clarence Ham • A civil engineer in the United States Air Force

Robin Harfouche • Global Revival

O.C. Harms • Pastor, Colonial Tabernacle / President of the California Evangelistic Association

Steve Harris • Horse Trainer

Lieutenant Commander Steve Harris • U.S. Navy, held prisoner for eleven months

Bob Harrison • Founder / Increase

John Harrison • Flavor developer for Dryer's and Edy's Grand Ice Cream

Mark Harfield • Senator from Oregon

Ron Haus • Pastor, President / TV 42

Norvel Hayes • Founder / Norvel Hayes Ministries

Jack Hayford • Chancellor / The Kings University

Orel Hershiser • Received baseball's Cy Young Award, the Championship Series MVP Award, and the World Series

Marilyn Hickey • President / Marilyn Hickey Ministries

Tommy Hicks • Evangelist

Benny Hinn • Pastor / Benny Hinn Ministries

Chico Holiday • Former Las Vegas nightclub entertainer

Sir Keith Holyoake • Governor / General in New Zealand

Darrell Hon • Real Estate developer / On Grandfather's Executive Committee

Cleve Howard • Master Sergeant / Communications at Camp Beale, Air Force Base

Rodney Howard-Browne • Founder / Revival Ministries International

Mary Hudson • President / Arise International

Rex Humbard • Evangelist

Charles and Frances Hunter • Evangelist / Known as The Happy Hunters

Daren E. Jack • United States Air Force Pilot

Glenda Jackson • Niece of Maria Woodworth-Etter, Glenda Jackson Ministries

Admiral Grady Jackson • Rear Admiral United States Navy

Major General John Jackson • United States Army

John Paul Jackson • Founder / Streams Ministries International

Judy Jacobs • Co-Pastor / Dwelling Place Church International

Tony Jansezian • Fellow Armenian from Jerusalem

James E. Johnson • Former Assistant Secretary of the Navy

Jeff Johnson • Senior Pastor / Calvary Chapel Downey

Dr. Rodney Johnson • Manager, Lunar & Interplanetary Systems Development for General Electric Co. / Responsible for development of space systems for manned exploration of the moon

Dean Jones • Actor /in That Darn Cat, The Love Bug, Beethoven, Golden Globe nominee

Noel Jones • Bishop / City of Refuge, Featured on Preachers of L.A.

Rick Joyner • MorningStar Ministries

Karen Kavorkian • Producer / Favor Films

Lieutenant Commander Arthur Keen • United States Navy

Gary Keesee • Pastor, Host / Fixing the Money Thing

Graham Kerr • Television personality / Host of "The Galloping Gourmet"

Zacchaeus Kibiubi • Translated the Bible into the Tharaka dialect

Ben Kinchlow • Host of The 700 Club

Honorable J. Byron Klaue • Chairman Board of Directors for Grandfather's organization

Patricia King • Co-Founder / XP Media

Henry Krause • A leading Plow Manufacturer / On Grandfather's Executive Committee

Ardian Kristanto • International Director & National President under Dad's Presidency, Executive Vice President under Mario Garcia, Indonesia; Chairman of IKA Group

Kathryn Kuhlman • Evangelist / She called herself an ordinary person used by God for extraordinary things. In 1974 on The Tonight Show, Johnny Carson said, "I find you fascinating."

Colonel Hank Lackey • Fighter Pilot

Paul Lai • International Director, USA, under my dad's Presidency; Taiwan; Hawaii

Louis LaMarr • Trial Lawyer / Former Professor of Law at John Marshall University

Marcus Lamb • CEO of Daystar Television Network / Evangelist

Tom Landry • Coach for the Dallas Cowboys football team

Major Robert B. Lantz • Chaplain / United States Air Force

Tom Leding • International Director, USA, under my dad's Presidency

Meadowlark Lemon • Of the Harlem Globetrotters

Carl Lewis • Olympic Champion winning four Gold Medals

Carman Licciardello • Recording Artist / Multiple GMA Dove Award Winner

Alf Liljehall • International Director, Sweden, under my dad's Presidency

Gordon Lindsay • Founder of Christ for the Nations Institute / Voice of Healing

Lieutenant A. E. Lloyd, Jr. • United States Navy

Mauricio Loucel. • Sec. of Global Advisory Council, President Universidad Tecnologica; El Salvador

Sir Lionel Luckhoo • Four times Mayor of Georgetown, Guyana and twice Knighted by Queen Elizabeth ll, Guinness Book of World Records as the most successful Criminal Attorney

Lynwood Maddox • Attorney / International Director of my grandfather's organization

General Fred Mahaffey • U.S. Army Four-Star General, Commander in Chief

Al Malachuk • A manufacturer's representative / Director for Grandfather's organization

Dan Malachuk • Logos Magazine publisher

Guillermo Maldonado • Apostle / King Jesus International Ministry

President Ferdinand Marcos • President of the Philippines

Ralph Marinacci • An early International Director for my grandfather's organization

Danny E. Mawuenyega • Exc. International Secretary, under my dad's Presidency, Ghana

Allen Mayer • Vice President of Oscar Mayer Company

Lieutenant Colonel James McAfee • United States Army

Bill McCartney • Head Football Coach University of Colorado

Sandy McDonnell • Chairman of McDonnell Douglas Aircraft manufacturing company

Roger McDuff • Speaker at my grandfather's organization

Ed McGlasson • All American football player four times / Played Pro with the New York Jets, Los Angeles Rams, New York Giants and Philadelphia Eagles

Ruckins McKinley, D.D. • Author / The Sound

Lieutenant Colonel Talmadge F. McNabb • United States Army

Aimee Semple McPherson • Pentecostal Evangelist

Dr. Jerre Melilli • An International Director for my grandfather's organization

Dick Mills • Evangelist

Len Mink • Evangelist / Musician

Chris Mitchell • Middle East Bureau Chief / CBN News

Sam Moore • R & B Singer Songwriter / Member of the Rock & Roll Hall of Fame / the Grammy Hall of Fame / Grammy Award winner / Multi Gold Record award-winning artist

Bob Mumford • Charismatic Teacher

Mike Murdock • Christian singer-songwriter / Pastor, The Wisdom Center

Mario Murillo • Evangelist

LT. JG. Paul D. Nealy • United States Navy

Bill Nelson • Congressman / Chairman of the House Sub-Committee on Space, trained for Nasa's space Shuttle Columbia flight

Thomas Nickel • Businessman

Joe Ninowski, Jr • Producer, Music Director, Writer / Daystar Television Network

Joe Ninowski, Sr. & his brother Dan • International Director of Grandfather's organization

President Richard Nixon • 37th President of the U. S. / 36th Vice-President of the U. S.

Norman Norwood • Home builder / Real estate developer

Ing. Mario Garcia Olvera • International Director under Dad's Presidency; Mexico
In 2018 he was elected the 3rd FGBMFI International President, after my dad..

Ricardo Oreamuno • International Director, Costa Rica, under my dad's Presidency

T. L. Osborn • Pentecostal Evangelist / Singer / Teacher

Charles Osborn • Father of T.L. Osborn

John and Dodie Osteen • Founders / Lakewood Church, Parents of Joel Osteen

Don Ostrom • Businessman

George Ottis • First layman invited to speak on U.S.S. Hancock / Owned Radio Stations

Francis Owusu • Int. Director under Dad and Mario Garcia's Presidency; Ghana; Hotelier

David Oyedepo • Bishop / Winners' Chapel International

Captain T. D. Parham • United States Navy

Rod Parsley • Pastor / World Harvest Church / Host of Breakthrough

Terri Copeland Pearsons • Senior Pastor / Eagle Mountain Church

Juan Manuel Pena • International Director, Nicaragua, under my dad's Presidency

Alberto Pereira • International Vice Treasurer under Mario Garcia's Presidency;
Agronomist & Attorney, Nicaragua

Chuck D. Pierce • President / Glory of Zion International

Commander David Plank • Chaplain, United States Naval Academy at Annapolis

Ron Potterbaum • A fellow Farmer

George Prah • International Director, Ghana, under my dad's Presidency

Charles Price • Evangelist

Frederick K.C. Price • Apostle / Ever Increasing Faith

Earl Prickett • Owned industrial tank maintenance Co., On Grandfather's Exec. Committee

Derek Prince • International Bible teacher / Former Professor at Cambridge University

Joseph Prince • Pastor / New Creation Church

Honorable Fidel Ramos • President of the Philippines

President Ronald Reagan • 40th President of the United States of America

William Standish Reed • Spirit-filled Surgeon / U.S. Navy medical officer

Dan Reeves • Former assistant to Coach Tom Landry / Head Coach Denver Broncos

Allen Rice • Professional football player, running back, with Minnesota Vikings and Green Bay Packers

Howard Richardson • Pastor, Prophet / Gates of Glory

Jeannie Riley • Known for her pop hit Harper Valley PTA

Richard Roberts • Oral Roberts Ministries

Oral Roberts • Founder / Oral Roberts Ministries and Oral Roberts University

Pat Robertson • Law degree from Yale University / Chancellor and CEO of Regent University / Founder of Christian Broadcasting Network

James Robison • Founder, LIFE Outreach International / Host of Life Today

Roy Rodgers & Dale Evans • Singers, Actors / Known as "King of the Cowboys"

Samuel Rodriguez • President / National Hispanic Christian Leadership Conference

Jimmy Rogers • Rogers Restaurant owner / President of Rogers-Woods & Associates

Jewel Rose • A farming rancher of Turkeys

Kyle Rote • New York Giants and the Houston Hurricanes

Sid Roth • Host / It's Supernatural!

David Rothschild • Pres. of Beverly Hills chapter of Grandfather's organization

Sam Rudd • Real Estate Developer in Colorado / Served under George Patton

Mark Rutland • Evangelist, President of Global Servants

President Anwar Sadat • President of Egypt

Fernando Samudio • International Director, Paraguay, under my dad's Presidency

Colonel Hans E. Sandrock • Exec. Director of the U. S. Armed Forced Chaplain Board

Ralph Sariejo • Television Producer / The Bionic Woman and Salvage 1 with Andy Griffith / Production manager on television series McMillan and Wife

Jerry Savelle • Founder / Jerry Savelle Ministries International

Ken and Annie Schisler • Face To Face Ministry

Robert Schuller • Founder of Crystal Cathedral, Radio show Hour of Power

Dianne Scott • My grandfather's Executive Secretary

Major Dutch Schultz • United States Air Force, flew combat in Vietnam

Lieutenant General Richard Shaefer • NATO Military Committee's International Staff

Lieutenant General Alonzo Short • Three-Star General / Director of Defense

Charles Simpson • Pastor / Bible Teacher

Chuck Smith • Pastor / Founded Calvary Chapel

Clayton E. Sonmore • Restauranteur

Del Sowerby, MD • Senior Anesthesiologist at Redding Medical Center

Dennis Spenst • International Director, Canada, under my dad's Presidency

Larry Stockstill • Pastor / Bethany World Prayer Center

Roy Stockstill • Founder / Bethany World Prayer Center

Tim Storey • Interviewed by Oprah Winfrey / OWN's Super Soul Sunday / Speaker

Dr. Jerome Stowell • Scientist

Bill Subritzky • Senior partner of New Zealand law firm, Director Home Building Co.

Lester Sumrall • Pentecostal Pastor and Evangelist

S.K. Sung • Organized grandfathers' Far East Airlift / President Hong Kong Chapter

Ronnie Svenhard • Swedish Bakery / International Director for Grandfather's organization

Bill Swad • Businessman, International Vice-President of Grandfather's organization

Honorable B.E. Talboys • Deputy Prime Minister of New Zealand

Ara Tavidjian • Regional Director for grandfather in Zurich, Switzerland / Close friend

Commander R. F. Thomas • United Stated Navy

Michael Thompson • Los Angeles Lakers

William Thompson • Chairman of Grandfather's British Committee in London Convention 1965

Nick Timko • Owner of Deluxe Die Works / On Grandfather's Executive Committee

Dennis Tinerino • "Mr. Universe"

Paul and Joyce Toberty • Authors / A Nation Born in a Day

A.C. Valdez • Evangelist

Shannon Vandruff • Upscale Builder of Cinderella Homes / Featured in Readers Digest

Simon Vikse • International Director of Grandfather's organization / Building Contractor

Maria von Trapp • Matriarch of the Trapp Family Singers, Subject of The Sound of Music

Jerry B. Walker •Ordained minister, International Pentecostal Holiness Church, Evangelist

General Lewis Walt • Four-Star General, Asst. Commandant, United States Marine Corps

William B. Walton • Co-Founder of Holiday Inn Hotels

Harvey Watson • Finance, Director for Grandfather's organization

James Watt • Former U.S. Secretary of the Interior

Scott Wead • Pastor / Life House Worship Center

Ron Weinbender • Presidential Envoy to my dad, Richard Shakarian

Dr. Don Whittaker • A renowned Surgeon

David Wilkerson • Author, The Cross and the Switchblade / Founder, Teen Challenge

Ralph Wilkerson • Founder / Melodyland Christian Center / Evangelist

Carl Williams • A noted Geologist, On Grandfather's Executive Committee

DeCarol Williamson • International Director, USA, under Grandfather's & Dad's Presidency

Lieutenant Commander Norman Winningham • U.S.S. Navy Aircraft Carrier Enterprise

Jerry Woodfill • NASA's Orbiter Experiment Mgr, Project Engineer for Apollo's warning systems, Presidential Medal of Freedom for the rescue of Apollo 13

Dan Wooding • Award-winning Journalist

Al Worthington • Braniff Airline Pilot, Played Major League Baseball; including Pitcher

Gary Zamora • Pastor / Gary Zamora Ministries

Efrem Zimbalist, Jr. • Actor; 77 Sunset Strip, The F.B.I., Maverick, Animated Iron Man & Batman series.

References

I had the great pleasure of hearing my Shakarian family stories numerous times over the course of my life. Most of the details of this book are a recounting of my memories of these stories, though I relied on the following sources to confirm the accuracy of some details. I also interviewed many people who knew my grandfather, attended his meetings or were touched by his organization. The book is compiled from actual events. The opinions expressed and the stories that were written are those of the author and do not necessarily reflect the views of others unless otherwise quoted.

Brown, C. (2010, December 30). Looking back on. . .The Shakarian Family. *The Downey Patriot*, p. 1.

Feder, B. J. (2002, July 18). I.B.M. beats forecasts but with signs of weakness. *The New York Times*, p. C1.

Photo by Ed Fuentes. Picture of Clifton's Cafeteria. With Permission and Courtesy of "USC Libraries. "Dick" Whittington Collection, 1924-1987", USC Libraries. Picture of Clifton's Cafeteria. All worldwide rights reserved.

Greitchen, Jeff. (2016, July 14) TBN World Headquarters. With Permission and Courtesy of THE ORANGE COUNTY REGISTER File Photo, All worldwide rights reserved.

Jensen, J. (1965, January). Son of Promise. Full Gospel Business Men's Voice. Los Angeles, CA: Full Gospel Business Men's Fellowship International.

Oliver, M. (1993, July 30). Demos Shakarian; Founded Religious Group. Los Angeles Times. Retrieved from http://articles.latimes.com/1993-07-30/news/mn-18417_1_demos-shakarian"articles.latimes.com/1993-07-30/news/mn-18417_1_demos-shakarian.

Nickel, T. (1964). The Shakarian Story. Full Gospel Business Mens Fellowship International, Los Angeles, CA.

Voices of the Military, Full Gospel Business Men's Fellowship International, Los Angeles, California

Roberts, O. (1965, January). His Works Do Follow Him. Full Gospel Business Men's Voice. Los Angeles, CA: Full Gospel Business Men's Fellowship International.

Henderson, J. (1963, April 3). Graham and ORU Draw Multitudes. Tulsa World, from http://www.tulsaworld.com/archives/graham-and-oru-draw-multitudes/article_c6637575-c4be-5ff9-b4f9-39bb5261b926.html.

Anonymous. (2005, January 25). Memories of living and working in Orange County, California. About Us; Orange County Memories. Retrieved from http://www.octhen.com.

Tributes To Isaac Shakarian. (1965, January). Full Gospel Business Men's Voice. Los Angeles, CA: Full Gospel Business Men's Fellowship International.

Reagan, R. (1984, July 5). Greeting from President Ronald Reagan; FGBMFI 31st International Convention, Anaheim, California. TBN; Praise The Lord. Retrieved from: http://www.itbn.org.

Jensen, J. (1993, October). Full Gospel Business Men's Voice. Costa Mesa, CA: Demos Shakarian Memorial Issue.

Clinton, B. (1993, July 3). Birthday message from President Bill Clinton; FGBMFI 40th International Convention, Boston, Massachusetts. Retrieved from: https://www.youtube.com.

Graham, Billy. (1962, October). Something is Happening. Full Gospel Business Men's Voice. Los Angeles, CA: Full Gospel Business Men's Fellowship International.

Carson, Ben. (1991, February). Gifted Hands. Full Gospel Business Men's Voice. Los Angeles, CA: Full Gospel Business Men's Fellowship International.

Shakarian, D. (1981, October 4). America For Jesus; Pasadena, California. TBN; Praise The Lord. Retrieved from http://www.itbn.org.

Shakarian, D. (1979, November). Full Gospel Business Men's Voice. Costa Mesa, CA: Who Am I? and Osteen, J. Victorious Living Series #22.

Shakarian, D., Sherrill, J., & Sherrill, E. (1975). The Happiest People on Earth. Ada, MI: Chosen Books.

Our Banner is Love. (1965, January). Full Gospel Business Men's Voice. Los Angeles, CA. Full Gospel Business Men's Fellowship International.

Osteen, J. Lakewood Church, Houston, Texas. Retrieved from: Joel Osteen Sermon.

Ghezzi, B. (1986, June). Demos Shakarian's Legacy, p. 7. Courtesy of Charisma Magazine, Ann Arbor, MI. Quotes are reprinted with permission from Charisma, June 1986. Copyright Charisma Media, USA. All rights reserved. www.charismamag.com.

Scriptures from; BibleGateway.com. Leviticus 22:20 New Life Version (NLV) Copyright © 1969 by Christian Literature International. Holy Bible, copyright © 1996, 2004, 2015. Used by permission of Tyndale House Publishers Inc.

Scripture Deuteronomy 28:1- 14. Holy Bible, New International Version®, NIV® Copyright ©1973, 1978, 1984, 2011 by Biblica, Inc.® Used by permission. All rights reserved worldwide.

Scripture 1 Corinthians 12:4-14. Holy Bible, New International Version®, NIV® Copyright ©1973, 1978, 1984, 2011 by Biblica,Inc.® Used by permission. All rights reserved worldwide.

About the Author

Cynthia Shakarian is an International Speaker
and Inspirational Author.

She is the granddaughter of Demos Shakarian.
In honor of her grandfather, Ms. Shakarian is continuing his legacy
and his humanitarian efforts through her organization,
"THE DEMOS SHAKARIAN FOUNDATION."
www.TDSF.org

Cynthia Shakarian is the author of the inspirational life story

How A Humble Dairyman Inspired The World!
DEMOS SHAKARIAN

"My dearest granddaughter Cynthia,
I see great things in you. God has blessed you
with the ability to relate to people from all walks of life.
Your compassionate heart and soft-spoken manner draw people in.
The gifts God has given you will impact nations!"
Love, Your Bobby
— Demos Shakarian

Contact Information
Hello@CynthiaShakarian.com
www.CynthiaShakarian.com
888-246-6003

CPSIA information can be obtained
at www.ICGtesting.com
Printed in the USA
BVHW071225140720
583604BV00001B/60